Images of Martinsville
Virginia

By Thomas D. Perry

History and Memory Series of Laurel Hill Publishing

ISBN: 1448644011
ISBN-13: EAN-139781448644018
Library of Congress Control Number: 2010904103

Laurel Hill Publishing
4443 Ararat Highway
P. O. Box 11
Ararat, VA 24053
freestateofpatrick@yahoo.com
www.freestateofpatrick.com

For Adam and Lauren,
who have bigger hearts than anyone I know.

Special Thanks to Elva Adams and Jerry Brock for their support and willingness to share their photos and history with this author. Unless noted otherwise, all images in this book come from the files of the Bassett Historical Center, our regional history library.

Also by Thomas D. Perry

Ascent To Glory: The Genealogy of J. E. B. Stuart

The Free State of Patrick: Patrick County Virginia In The Civil War

J. E. B. Stuart's Birthplace: The History of the Laurel Hill Farm

Notes From The Free State Of Patrick:
Patrick County, Virginia, and Regional History

"North Carolina Has Done Nobly": J. E. B. Stuart's North Carolina Connections

God's Will Be Done: The Christian Life of J. E. B. Stuart

Patrick County Oral History Project: A Guide

J. E. B. Stuart's Birthplace: A Guide for Educators and Visitors

Upward Toil: The Lester Family of Henry County Virginia

Images of Patrick County Virginia

Images of Mount Airy, North Carolina

Visit www.freestateofpatrick.com for more information

Table of Contents

About Thomas D. Perry

J. E. B. Stuart's biographer Emory Thomas describes Tom Perry as "a fine and generous gentleman who grew up near Laurel Hill, where Stuart grew up, has founded J. E. B. Stuart Birthplace and attracted considerable interest in the preservation of Laurel Hill. He has started a symposium series about aspects of Stuart's life to sustain interest in Stuart beyond Ararat, Virginia." Perry holds a BA in History from Virginia Tech in 1983.

Tom started the J. E. B. Stuart Birthplace Preservation Trust, Inc. in 1990. The non-profit organization preserved 75 acres of the Stuart property including the house site where James Ewell Brown Stuart was born on February 6, 1833. Perry wrote the eight interpretive signs about Laurel Hill's history along with the Virginia Civil War Trails sign and the new Virginia Historical Highway Marker in 2002. He spent many years researching traveling all over the nation to find Stuart materials including two trips across the Mississippi River to visit nearly every place "Jeb" Stuart served in the United States Army (1854-1861).

Tom can be seen on Virginia Public Television's Forgotten Battlefields: The Civil War in Southwest Virginia with his mentor noted Civil War Historian Dr. James I. Robertson, Jr. Perry has begun a collection of papers relating to Stuart and Patrick County history in the Special Collections Department of the Carol M. Newman Library at Virginia Tech under the auspices of the Virginia Center For Civil War Studies.

In 2004, Perry began the Free State Of Patrick Internet History Group, which has become the largest historical organization in the area with over 500 members. It covers Patrick County Virginia and regional history. Tom produces a monthly email newsletter about regional history entitled Notes From The Free State of Patrick that goes from his website www.freestateofpatrick.com.

In 2009, Perry donated proceeds to the Bassett Historical Center, where he hosts a regional history symposium each March, from his book Images of America: Henry County Virginia. This book along with the Henry County Heritage Book that Perry edited generated over $50,000 to expand the regional history library.

Introduction

The logo says "Martinsville, A City Without Limits," but did you know that while the city looks to the future, its history begins before the American Revolution. General Joseph Martin, shown in an image on the next page lends his name to the city of Martinsville, while his more famous contemporary, Patrick Henry, lends his name to the county surrounding the city.

Martinsville sits in the middle of Henry County named for Virginia's first governor, Patrick Henry, the orator of the American Revolution. Best known for this famous statement, "Give me liberty or give me death," Henry lived in the eastern section of the county called Leatherwood. Today, when you look at a map of Virginia, you read his name Patrick Henry as this author's native county, which was once part of Henry County, also received the name of the famous firebrand of revolution.

Patrick Henry (1736-1799) was the first governor of Virginia 1776-79 and the sixth governor 1784-86. During the years in between his separate terms leading the Commonwealth of Virginia, Henry lived in Henry County named for him in 1776. His 10,000-acre farm grew tobacco with slave labor. Called Leatherwood, it was just east of present day Martinsville far from the war although Cornwallis during the Guilford Courthouse Campaign, "The Race for the Dan River," did come close in 1781.

Joseph Martin (1740-1808), often described as the "Forgotten Man of the Revolution" hailed from Albemarle County, but first came to the area that bears his name in 1773. He bought land on the Smith River in present day Henry County, but Halifax County when purchased.

Martin was the son of Joseph Martin, Sr., who was the first of his family to come to America, and Susannah Chiles. They had seven children until her death by smallpox in 1782.

Martin served in the French and Indian War at Fort Pitt, present day Pittsburgh, Pennsylvania, in 1756. He served with Thomas Sumter of South Carolina, who had the fort that started the Civil War over a hundred years later named for him.

Martin standing over six feet was described as a "rough around the edges." He had a heavy build with a full beard and balding. At times he braided his beard and tucked into his shirt. In formal company, he wore knee breeches and buckled shoes later in life, but as a young man he was a "Long Hunter" made famous by Daniel Boone and others, but Martin was Boone before Boone.

When three or four men went out in the fall to hunt going over 100 miles beyond the settlements in East Tennessee, which resulted in capture by the Indians among other adventures. Martin, encouraged by Dr. Thomas Walker, a friend and neighbor of Thomas Jefferson, explored the Powell Valley in present day Tennessee ahead of Daniel Boone in the 1760s. In 1774, Royal Governor Dunmore appointed him Captain of the Pittsylvania Militia, which included present day Henry County. He built forts near Cumberland Gap and as Cornwallis came through the south on his way to Guilford Courthouse and defeat at Yorktown, Martin helped keep the Natives from attacking the patriots. Patrick Henry appointed Martin as Indian Agent in 1777. In 1781, he served in the Virginia and North Carolina legislatures along with settling the dispute between North Carolina and the "Free State of Franklin" in 1788 over possible statehood.

In 1784, Martin married Susannah Graves, a neighbor on the Smith River. He had eleven children with her. Martin reportedly had an Indian wife, Betsy Ward. Overall, Martin had at least 23 children and 40 grandchildren, which gives him descendants all over the country today.

The following year in 1785 came another appointment to make a treaty with the Cherokees and other tribes came along. In 1787, Martin went to Georgia to make a treaty with the Creek Indian Nation and spent several years there enough to receive election to the Georgia Legislature in 1793. He returned to Virginia, where Robert E. Lee's father, Henry "Light Horse Harry" Lee, appointed him Brigadier General of the 12th Brigade of Virginia Militia during the "Whiskey Rebellion."

In the 1790s, Martin served for eight years in the Virginia Legislature. He worked to settle the boundary dispute between Kentucky and Virginia in 1795. In 1802, he did the same along the border between Virginia and Tennessee.

In 1804, he retired and returned to a new home on Leatherwood Creek. In 1808, Martin made a last trip to his lands in the west and returned exhausted to Leatherwood Creek in present day Henry County, where he died on December 18, 1808.

Martinsville sits in the piedmont of Virginia along the border with North Carolina. After the Civil War, this region was the tobacco belt where families such as the Reynolds and Penns of neighboring Patrick County formed businesses for chewing tobacco that evolved into R. J. Reynolds and American Tobacco Company. Henry County contributed its own tobacco brand names from the Lester and Gravely families.

With the coming of the railroads before the turn of the twentieth century, distribution of products such as furniture led to the formation of companies that became American, Bassett, Hooker, and Stanley Furniture Companies. This was followed by the growth of textiles such as Sale Knitting below along with Pannill Knitting and Tultex.

    In the mid-1900s, the Smith River was a source of devastating floods until harnessed with the building of Philpott Dam and Reservoir. This allowed even more industrialization and electrical power that fueled growth in Martinsville. Today, the river is a source of recreation and still gives power to the region and the city of Martinsville.

The descendants of Joseph Martin still come back home to Henry County and the city that bears their name. Recently, these portraits of Colonel Joseph Martin (1785-1859), the son of General Joseph Martin, and his wife, Sarah Hughes Martin (ca.1791-1883), according to Pannill Martin returned to the Bassett Historical Center, the regional history library in the Blue Ridge Regional Library System for all to see the family that gives Martinsville its name.

Virginia formed Henry County from neighboring Pittsylvania County at the end of 1776 including lands that today are Patrick and Franklin Counties. In 1791, George Hairston donated fifty acres of land that became Martinsville. In 1824, the second courthouse structure went up downtown and was renovated several times before the county moved its government to north of Collinsville in the late twentieth century. Martinsville grew up around the courthouse until 1929 when it became an independent city separating from Henry County. Twenty years later the city began using the City Manager type of government taking the operating power from the mayor.

This book hopes to give visitors and natives a glimpse into the past along with a view of the present with some thoughts on the future of Martinsville, Virginia. It is not a definitive history nor meant to portray everyone and everything of importance that occurred in the "City Without Limits," but to simply give interested parties a place to learn and remember the history and people of Martinsville and Henry County, Virginia. It is a snapshot of time, both good and bad. History and heritage are not the sole privy of censors or archivists. History and images belong to everyone and that is what this book hopes to convey.

Each year Martinsville welcomes tourists from all over the nation especially twice for NASCAR races. History is part of efforts to revitalize the area around the courthouse square. Even the Commonwealth of Virginia get it wrong sometimes as shown in the historical highway marker below that states incorrectly that Stoneman came to the "City Without Limits." It was William J. Palmer in cómmand of the cavalry under the overall command of Stoneman. Behind the marker is the old Kearfott Drug Store, better known to some as the "Dreamcycle Building."

Chapter One
"Greetings From Martinsville, Virginia"
Postcards

Deltiology or the collecting of postcards is a hobby everywhere even in Martinsville and Henry County, Virginia. From the time of Queen Victoria of Britain through World War I the "Greetings From" was the primary type of postcard. So to the reader, this book begins with "Greetings from Martinsville, Virginia."

Postcards trace their history back to the Civil War in which General Stuart fought and gave his life. Hand drawn images of battlefields by artists such as William Henry Jackson began to appear in 1862. Nine years later the U. S. Post Office preprinted stamps on the cards and continued the practice until 1898. These cards had one side for the address and one side for the message. Major events such as the 1893 Chicago World's Fair gave visitors a reason to mail home a postcard. Five years after that event, Private Mail Cards or PMC came into use authorized by the U. S. Congress and three years later in 1901 the term postcard came into being. The "Undivided Back Era" lasted until March 1907. These postcards had space for the message with the image on one side and the address on the other.

From 1907 through 1915, addresses and space for the message were on one side and an image on the other. Germany printed most of these cards of the "Divided Back or Golden Era," but with World War I that changed. From the end of that war until 1930 when the "Blue Sky Era" printers released postcards with white borders around the images and scenes had blue sky added to them on postcards. In 1930, a linen feel came into use on the cards that lasted for thirty years. Just before World War II, the "Real Photo Post Cards" or "Chrome" we know today came into use.

The following two pages show churches and schools from Martinsville's past. Starting with postcards of the churches in Martinsville is always a good idea. The Baptist, Presbyterian, and Methodists are just some of the sects of the Christian faith that also includes Episcopalians. Martinsville, like many independent cities, has its own school system. The next page shows three postcards from schools in that system from the past.

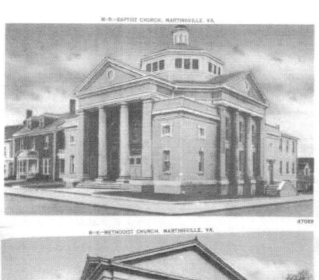

High School Building,
Martinsville, Va.

New High School, Martinsville, Va.

North Martinsville 1935

Tourism in the twenty-first century became a vital part of the economy. These postcards represent the boom with the coming of the automobile even though I do not believe either motel is really in Martinsville in spite of their labels, but in neighboring Collinsville. This boom in the time of the automobile included two NASCAR races every year that still pump millions into the local economy providing a stable infusion twice a year in tough economic times.

Forest Park Golf Course sits on the land formerly called the Lanier Farm at one time owned by Henry Clay Lester and his heirs in the Rives Brown Family. Chatmoss, once a home of the Hairston family, is now a private country club and residential area in Martinsville.

On the following page are postcards from Martinsville Hospitals. The sale of the Martinsville and Henry County Memorial Hospital generated millions of dollars that the Harvest Foundation beginning in 2002 distributes to worthwhile projects on health, education, and welfare. One of their matching grants was $200,000 to the Bassett Historical Center in 2009 for expansion of the building.

The Shackelford Hospital, Martinsville, Virginia.

By Reed Photo Company.

The Martinsville General Hospital, Martinsville, Va.

Henry County Memorial Hospital, Martinsville, Va.

Chapter Two
Elva's Chapter

      This entire chapter is courtesy of Elva Adkins Adams and her website www.mymartinsville.com or www.myhenrycounty.com. Elva is a strong supporter of positive people and things in Martinsville and Henry County. She came from Fieldale and calls them like she sees them. This author appreciates her support and here are some of the historic images from her collection.

      Below left and middle are Thomas Everette and Sally Eggleston Adkins. Their son Herbert Otis "Hub" Adkins (1918-1985), shown below right, married nineteen year old Margaret Pearl Price in 1941 and the next year their first child, a daughter named Elva, joined the population of Henry County. Two more children Susan and Truman followed after "Hub" returned from war in Italy.

      Margaret Pearl Price Adkins, far right celebrating a bowling victory over her daughter, Elva, is the daughter of John and Ethel Shull Price, shown left and middle below. Margaret is also the author of *Echoes*, a collection of her short stories.

Here are the Shackelford daughters of Dr. and Mrs. John A. Shackelford around 1950. Left to right, they are Margaret, Mary Williamson, Blanche Harrison, and Frances. Below, Dr. John A. Shackelford, who along with his father, Dr. Jesse Shackelford, M.D., operated a hospital on Church Street in Martinsville. The hospital founded in 1921 was originally the home of the Teague family and was located approximately where Draper and Ferrell Clothing is today. Sold in 1946, the hospital relocated to the Starling Avenue site and became the Martinsville General Hospital. Dr. John Shackelford was born November 30, 1893 in Irisburg and died February 5, 1956, in Baltimore, Maryland. (Courtesy of Elva Adams, www.myhenrycounty.com)

Every year Elva's website recognizes people who make a difference. Ruby Davis was the 2009 Volunteer of the Year. "Ruby is likely one of the busiest people you know. It seems to me she is volunteering every day of the week somewhere. Whether it is Tackfully Teamed and taking care of the horse barn or garden club or Friends of the Library, she is a worker. Here she is at the Friends Used Book Sale which happens several times a year. Ruby and her gang of helpers sort and shelve books to sell for only a little bit of money. But the money adds up to be a great help to operations at the Blue Ridge Regional Library. Thanks Ruby for all you do!" (Courtesy of Elva Adams, www.myhenrycounty.com) Below, Ruby with George Dyer at one of the many Friends of the Library sales held throughout the year. George, a former FBI man and Vietnam Veteran is a frequent visitor to the sales. (Courtesy of Ruby Davis.)

Elva named Jennifer Doss as her website's Person of the Year 2009. "Here's Jennifer on site with a member of the construction crew as the last bit of bridge steel is removed in Fieldale. I first met Jennifer when I emailed her asking for copies of the Fieldale Bridge photos. The next thing I knew I was part of the bridge committee. And soon I found I had donated money for a memorial plaque! Such is Jennifer's power over people: her enthusiasm is very contagious! She has been Rivers and Trails project manager for the Dan River Basin Association for two years. In December the Martinsville & Henry County Economic Development Corp. realized just how good she is: they named her the Director of Tourism for Martinsville and Henry County." Another person recognized by Elva was Beverly Yeager, who contributed multiple stories to the Henry County Heritage Book. Below is Beverly Lipford on the right with her sisters in 1940 at Fairystone State Park. (Courtesy of Elva Adams, www.myhenrycounty.com)

Here is Otis Bolejack with a captured momento of war. Otis
served in the Pacific Theatre with the Marines during WWII. He was
a native of Henry County, VA and he was married to Hazel Price and
had one daughter, Vicky. He had several brothers - Emory and Ed and
several sisters. After the war he worked at Fieldcrest Mills, the
Martinsville Police Department, and DuPont. Here he is with a
captured Japanese flag. (Courtesy of Elva Adams,
www.myhenrycounty.com)

Ruth Lawing on the left worked for many years as a
Registered Nurse at Martinsville General Hospital on Starling and
Memorial Hospital on Hospital Drive. Acting Director of Nursing
Mary Simmons Willis presents her with a service plaque. The date of
this photo is unknown but a good guess is about 1970. The plaque
commemorated forty-two years of service. (Courtesy of Elva Adams,
www.myhenrycounty.com)

Here are Ann Spencer and Jenny Harris in 1948. "Look over the existing bridge as you cross the Smith on 220 business south of Martinsville you will see these stone structures. They've been there a long time. The stone supports were part of the old covered bridge in that spot. The Harris family lived nearby on the other side of the bridge, and that house was torn down when Memorial Boulevard was built in the late 40s." Below is the covered bridge that spanned the Smith River in 1911. (Courtesy of Elva Adams, www.myhenrycounty.com)

(Courtesy of Elva Adams, www.myhenrycounty.com)

One of two major railroad lines coming through Martinsville was the Danville and Western, the "Dick and Willie," which ran from Danville and reached Stuart in 1884. The last train left Patrick County in 1942, thirty years after the above photo of Leaksville Station was taken in 1912. (Courtesy of Elva Adams, www.myhenrycounty.com)

Samuel Webster Adams III and William Chambliss Adams in the mid-1950s. Sam and Bill, the children of Samuel and Catherine Chambliss Adams, lived on Rives Road in Martinsville. (Courtesy of Elva Adams, www.myhenrycounty.com)

On June 26, 1959, the Martinsville High School Class of 1939 held its twentieth reunion. Pictured left to right first row: Ingles Ford Childress, Helen Ford Taylor, R.A. Henderson, Sallie Mason Clark (class sponsor), Norris Prillaman Miller, Mary Evelyn Shumate Spencer; second row: Christine Lester Sowden, Zada Prillaman Oakes, Dorothy Cummings Vogler, Vivian Kellam Powell, Gladys Brown Wyatt, Marie Gover Weaver, Sara Minter, Ida Richardson Deaton; third row: Roy Hodnett, Constance Adkins, Richard Prillaman, Melvin Wells, Dorothy Minter Corum, Janice Moore Martin, Louise Campbell Summers, Rose Pharis Cahill, and Harold Kolodny. (Courtesy of Elva Adams, www.myhenrycounty.com)

The Martinsville High School Class of 1912 includes standing, left to right: Hubert Smith, Mamie Hodges (Mrs. Sam Tuggle), Rebecca Kearfott (Mrs. Sam Carriel), Ruth Jones, Irving M. Groves, Sr., Laura Butler (Mrs. Tom Moore), Kathleen Teague (Mrs. T. R. Carter), Sallie Minter (Mrs. Lewis Hedgecock), John A. Shackelford; Seated, left to right: Jessie Clark (Mrs. B.W. Foster), Blanche Walker (Mrs. Peter S. Ford), Dillard Smith (Mrs. Edgar Boatwright), Elsie DeShazo, Mattie Hundley (Mrs. Irving Groves, Sr.). (Courtesy of Elva Adams, www.myhenrycounty.com)

The Martinsville High School Cheerleaders riding on/in a 1955 Chevy convertible pass by Wampler's Drugs on Main Street in Martinsville. Graves Wampler, who first worked at Patterson's Drugs on the courthouse square, operated Wampler's. About 1951, Wampler opened a small store on Main Street near Abe Globman's new department store. When Mr. Globman expanded so did Wampler. Another Wampler, Corky, was part of the business by the time of this photo. The man in the white shirt in the window looks like Graves Wampler. The cheerleaders in front of Wampler's were our Junior Varsity Cheerleaders: Mary Garland LaPrade, Patsy Ramsey, Barbara Cotty, Betsy Carper, Kay Isley, and Bonnie Stone. Miss Martinsville 1955 was Claudia Davis in that same 1955 Christmas Parade riding in a Ford. Driving the Ford is Jim Eanes, an announcer at WHEE. (Courtesy of Elva Adams, www.myhenrycounty.com)

"Marietta Warren was born in Rockingham County, N.C. on April 10, 1918. She was the daughter of George Dillard Warren (1879-1939) and Lena Alice Hundley Warren (1895-1975). She lived most of her youth on Beckham Church Road in Henry County, VA. She married Floyd William "Bill" Smith about 1935. She graduated from the Southern School of Beauty Culture in Norfolk, attended Boyd's School of Commerce, George Washington University, and Patrick Henry Community College. During her career, she worked for the Jobbers Pants Company, Rae's Beauty Salon, in the civil service with the Navy in Washington, DC during World War II, was secretary to the late Dr. Francis Teague for 25 years, and worked in the Spanish Lab at Patrick Henry Community College for 3 years. She was a member of McCabe Memorial Baptist Church since 1940 where she served as music director for 35 years, Sunday school teacher for more than 60 years, was also organist, pianist, choir director, and church historian. She was a sweet and very special lady. Marietta died June 3, 2008 and is buried in Oakwood Cemetery in Martinsville." (Courtesy of Elva Adams, www.myhenrycounty.com)

The Youth Choir of the First Baptist Church of Martinsville around 1946. First Row: Sue James, Beverly Lipford, Martha Ann Owen, Carolyn Thompson, Hope Hensley, Bobby Wheeler. Second Row: Unidentified, Carolyn Briggs, Patsy Barbour, Jimmy Simpson, Randolph Wheeler, Owen, Charlotte Bowen, Shirley Key, Margaret Turner, Carlene Hedgecock. Third Row: Frank Zentmeyer, Benny Eanes, Buzz Nowlin, Banks Via, John Palmer, Kay Rist, Billy Kirk, Harry Hensley, Gene McDaniel, Grace Hensley, Betty Lou Isley. Fourth Row: Buddy Stump, Johnny Hooker, Edwin Via, Joe Harris, David Doss, Susan Field, Sue Burch, Sara Grogan, Tommy Moses, Dottie Goodman. Fifth Row: Bobby Kirk, Johanna Land, Shirley Duncan, Catherine Hite, and Betty Stultz. (Courtesy of Elva Adams, www.myhenrycounty.com)

"Abe Globman was a Russian Jewish immigrant, who first arrived in Philadelphia in 1911. He moved to Martinsville in 1915 when he was 20 years old and bought a 2000 square foot store on the Square in uptown Martinsville. He married Mamie "Masha" Zimmerman shortly afterwards. With much hard work by the couple, the store expanded and in 1944 Globman spent $41,000 on the future Church Street site of his store. That store officially opened May 11, 1950, and was very successful. He expanded eight years later, buying the Presbyterian Church next door, and the Baptist Church across the street. His grandson, Barry Greene, described Globman as the only Jew in the world that owned two Christian churches. By 1951, his was one of the largest department stores in two states and he was "The Merchant Prince." Abe died in 1979, Masha in 1984. Sadly, the next year both of their children, Leon and Sissy, also died. The store suffered and eventually followed the route of other family owned department stores in closing. At its peak, Globman's consisted of four Globman's Department Stores and ten Lots of Labels Stores." (Courtesy of Elva Adams, www.myhenrycounty.com)

Jerry Blankenship, known to Martinsville residents as an organist, is an interior decorator and the owner of Elegant Design on Church Street. Here he is as a very young boy posing on a pony in Baltimore, Maryland. (Courtesy of Elva Adams, www.myhenrycounty.com)

    George Dillard Warren (1879-1939) and his wife Lena Alice Hundley Warren (1895-1975). They were married in Henry County on March 10, 1912. George was the son of Columbus Swanson Warren (1841-1925) and Mary Catherine Oakes Warren (1845-1915). Lena was the daughter of Joseph Taylor Hundley (1862-1949) and Mary Etta Hopkins Hundley (1863-1955). George was a painter by trade. George and Lena had three daughters: Marietta, Mildred, and Catherine. The family lived on Beckham Church Road many years before moving to N. Moss Street in Martinsville. They were musicians: George played the fiddle and Lena played the banjo. They entertained friends and neighbors by playing music in their home. Catherine would sell chewing gum to those in attendance listening to the music. George suffered poor health and died in 1939. First buried at Beckham Methodist Church, he later was moved to Oakwood Cemetery in Martinsville. Lena remarried about 1942 but this marriage did not work out and soon ended in divorce. Lena later cared for a sick brother, and her father and mother in their old age. She is buried in Oakwood Cemetery next to George." (Courtesy of Elva Adams, www.myhenrycounty.com)

This enlargement shows Martinsville tobacco magnate, E. J. Davis, at the Annual Convention of the Tobacco Association of the U.S. on June 26th, 1925, at Jamestown Island, Virginia. Mr. Davis operated the Banner Warehouse on Franklin Street for more than 40 years. Fire destroyed the warehouse in 1951. (Courtesy of Elva Adams, www.myhenrycounty.com)

This business shown about 1980 was located across from the old Bob White Chevrolet dealership on East Church Street in Martinsville, recycled hubcaps. Labeled "The Nut House," many as "Hub Cap City" knew it. (Courtesy of Elva Adams, www.myhenrycounty.com)

The First Baptist Church was located on the corner of Church and Broad Streets in Martinsville. The building to the left is the Church Parsonage and the building to the right is the Henry Hotel. The Church torn down to create a parking lot was rebuilt on Starling Avenue. (Courtesy of Elva Adams, www.myhenrycounty.com)

View of uptown Martinsville looking down Franklin Street in 1901. Banner Warehouse and Alliance Warehouse stood where the Franklin Street Parking Lot is today. They burned in 1951. Label at top by Heck Ford. (Courtesy of Elva Adams, www.myhenrycounty.com)

Martinsville General Hospital was located on Starling Avenue north of the First Baptist Church. It served the area from the 1940s to the 1960s. It became a nursing home after the new Hospital was built. (Courtesy of Elva Adams, www.myhenrycounty.com)

Admiral Richard Byrd (1888-1957) visited Martinsville and landed his Trimotor in a field in the Forest Park area. The exact year of this photo is unknown. Byrd of the famous Virginia family was one of the first to fly the Atlantic Ocean and explored the North and South Poles. He received the Medal of Honor for his service to the United States. (Courtesy of Elva Adams, www.myhenrycounty.com)

Taken in 1971 is the 50th Anniversary photo of the Charter Members of the Martinsville, Kiwanis Club Charter Members. Front row (L to R): J.R. Gregory, J. Frank Wilson, Irving M. Groves, Sr., S.F. Childress. Back row (L to R): W. P. Hodnett, Nick Prillaman, Sr., H.G. Moore, Sr. (Courtesy of Elva Adams, www.myhenrycounty.com)

Officers and directors of the Kiwanis Club in 1921-22, from left to right: Standing -- R. P. Gravely (Sr.), district trustee; H. A. Ford, A. L. Tuggle, Dr. H. V. Price. Sitting -- J. R. Gregory, E. J. Davis, J. E. Howard, president; John. W. Carter, Jr., secretary; T. F. Burch. (Courtesy of Elva Adams, www.myhenrycounty.com)

The Martinsville Rotary Club of 1928. Seated front left to right: G.T. Lester, Bill Turner, Garland LaPrade, Bob Atkins, Irvin Ramsey, Emmett Stover, Alex Wilson, and Dr. Charlie Reed. Standing left to right: Dr. Ran Smith, Jake Aaron, Harry Byrd, Dick Jones, Branch Rives, Dr. Eugene McDaniel, Dr. Burt Rush, Johnny Richardson, Ed Zentmeyer, Irvin Cubine, Unknown, Harry Nunn, Holladay Yeaman, Unknown, Dutch Chewning, S. L. Goodman, Unknown, and C.T. Fleenor. (Courtesy of Elva Adams, www.myhenrycounty.com)

Lavinder Springs and Store were once the crossroads of Martinsville. Citizens and travelers watered at the springs, located where Moorefield Cleaners and Laundry is now situated on Memorial Boulevard near Bridge Street. This photo shows a group assembled for the cameraman in front of Lavinder's Store about 1899. On the porch are J.B.C. Ambrose, founder of the Henry Bulletin; Powhatan Daniels, businessman; Mrs. Lavinder and Mr. Lavinder. E.F. Holt is in the wagon and T.C. Bouldin is standing beside it. The women are unidentified. (Courtesy of Elva Adams, www.myhenrycounty.com)

Here is Owen Hall in the WMVA radio studio, where he was news director from 1968 until he passed in January 1990. His children still hear from people especially about how he read letters to Santa Claus from local children. (Courtesy of Elva Adams, www.myhenrycounty.com) Below is Lynwood Judkins at WMVA in 1962, who was also a ham radio operator with the call numbers K4VBU. (Courtesy of Fred Bow.)

"Lucy Thompson Soyars Lipford was the mother of William Pleasant Lipford and the grandmother of B. C. Lipford of Martinsville. Lucy Soyars' grandfather was James Soyars of Halifax County and fought in the Revolutionary War, rising to the rank of Corporal. He was wounded in 1780, captured, and later was released due to disability. Having served under General Lafayette, he was one of the committee of reception during the French General's last visit to America in 1824. John married his second wife, Jane Oakes, on December 16, 1792, in Pittsylvania County. Their son, Pleasant Soyars, born May 30, 1799, in Pittsylvania County, married Mary (Polly) Coleman October 17, 1822, in Pittsylvania County. Pleasant and Mary had seven children among them was Lucy Thompson Soyars, born April 11, 1826, in Pittsylvania County. She married William R. Lipford on February 16, 1846, in Whitmell. Lucy had a son, John Daniel Lipford, and a daughter, Mary Elizabeth Lipford. William R. Lipford served in the Civil War in Captain William H. Rice's Company, 5th Battalion. In the 1880 census they were living in the Tunstall District, having bought 55 ½ acres of land there in 1876. Lucy lost her husband to a falling tree during a storm in 1896. Lucy applied for a Civil War Widows Pension, which she received. She and her unmarried daughter, nicknamed Molly, and then lived with her son John Daniel Lipford and his wife, Martha Hiler Lipford. They called Lucy "Little Grandmother." Lucy and daughter Molly were listed twice in the 1900 census, both in the Tunstall District. In the 1910 census, she and Molly were living with her son John and family in the Mayfield Precinct of Rockingham County, North Carolina. Lucy Soyars Lipford died May 12, 1912." (Courtesy of Elva Adams, www.myhenrycounty.com)

Joseph Taylor Hundley (1862-1949) was born in Henry County on January 17, 1862. He was the son of Granville Madison Hundley (1823-1862) and Louisa Odle Hundley (1821-after 1900). He was the grandson of John Hundley (1774-1850/60) of Henry County. He married Mary Etta Hopkins (1863-1955) on December 8, 1885, in Henry County. Joe and Mary Etta had 10 children; Rosa Bell (1886-1978), Mary Anne (1888-1984), Sallie Lou (1890-1968), Taylor Marshall (1891-1972), George Andrew (1893-1953), Lena Alice (1895-1975), Ramey Davis (1897-1991), Reid Lincoln (1900-1980), Joseph Sanders (1903-1990), and Bessie Ellen Hundley (1906-2007). This Hundley family lived in the Carlisle area of Henry County for many years on the "Worth place." They attended Centenary Church on the other side of Leatherwood Creek. Joe farmed much of his life. He worked at Fieldcrest Mills in Fieldale after he got too old to farm. Later they lived in Martinsville. Joe posed for this picture in the 1940s, but never actually rode a motorcycle. He died in Martinsville on May 2, 1949. Joe and Mary Etta rest today at Oakwood Cemetery in Martinsville. (Courtesy of Elva Adams, www.myhenrycounty.com)

This photograph taken at Liberty Heights Swimming Pool about 1948 seems to be a group from the Martinsville City Day Camp. Day Camp was held at the Martinsville City Park. We would take a bag lunch and had great times there. After lunch a bus took us to Liberty Heights Swimming Pool for the afternoon. Included in the group were Beverly Altschull, Claudia Davis, Betsy Tuggle, Boo Hooker, Dell Lacy, Beverly Lehman, Betsy Webb, Mary Garland LaPrade, and Beverly Lipford. Liberty Heights Pool built as a reservoir for fire protection for Lester Lumber Company in the 1920s was officially opened 4 July 1926. It closed in 1957 and was demolished August 1987 to make way for Liberty Fair Mall. The pool looked rather like a Roman Coliseum and had three rings of water. The outer ring was shallow for infants. The middle ring was four feet deep, and the inner ring was deep with a diving platform. There were two diving boards, one lower, and one higher. A large deck was for sunbathing and dancing, and there was a concession stand. Dressing rooms and lockers were downstairs. (Courtesy of Elva Adams, www.myhenrycounty.com)

Above, Saul Schreibfeder a relative of many of the local Jewish families including the Fusfelds and Kolodnys ran Jobbers Pants Factory and was instrumental in hiring black women to work in the factory. Below, described is a "One-Man Chamber of Commerce," Hezekiah "Heck" Ford, an "extraordinarily civic-minded man with deep family roots in Martinsville" as his great-grandfather was Col. Joseph Martin. Ford brought industry to replace the tobacco factories including Pannill Knitting. (Courtesy of Elva Adams, www.myhenrycounty.com)

Always wearing a hat, above, is Virginia Finley Whitener, who has stayed alive for over 100 years by walking a different path. This photo was taken at the YMCA where she walks. (Courtesy of Elva Adams, www.myhenrycounty.com)

If you lived five lifetimes you might learn as much as Polly Randolph knows. For the last forty years we've been amazed at the extent of her interests and knowledge. History, nature, birds, whatever, just name it. She can talk intelligently to anyone about anything. She has spent her life giving and volunteering. At age 94 in July 2009, she has touched many lives and they are all better for it. Polly, the granddaughter of Matthew Fontaine Maury, was married to attorney Cary Randolph. She has two daughters. She worked tirelessly for the Red Cross for years and in the early days of the Piedmont Arts Association. (Courtesy of Elva Adams, www.myhenrycounty.com)

My friend, Elva Adkins Adams, supplied the photos for this entire chapter. She works with the Friends of the Library. Her website www.myhenrycounty.com is one of the best sources for local history around. Below is one of the best photos from Martinsville of the courthouse square in 1905. Notice the stairs that do not exist today going up to the main courtroom. Fayette Street begins just to the left of the building.

Chapter Three
Downtown

Mapmakers calculate mileage from the post office in any given town, which makes this building ground zero for Martinsville, Virginia. Just across from the post office is the visitor's center on Church Street, a great place to start your visit to Martinsville. This book continues in this chapter with more images of the business hub of Martinsville in the downtown area. Once thriving, this area is now the focus of much rejuvenation and restoration stressing education with the New College Institute around the courthouse square. Below is the post office before 1930.

FULLER TIRE COMPANY INC. - 114 W. Church Street - Martinsville, Virginia - Ph. 632-3461

To get there many people used the tires sold at Fuller Tire Company shown above in another postcard. They might have paid from their account in the New Peoples Bank, the first bank building downtown that today still sits across the street from the old courthouse and New College Institute. Peoples Bank opened in 1891 when gas lamps were in use, lighted by W. R. Mills for $5 per month.

The New Peoples Bank,
Martinsville, Va.

One of the new hubs for visitors in downtown Martinsville is the Virginia Museum of Natural History, which began in 1984 as the Boaz Foundation. In 2007, the museum moved into a "world class facility" in Martinsville after many years in a local school. Affiliated with the Commonwealth of Virginia's Secretary of Natural Resources, this attraction gives the area a new tourism and educational facility. Below, schoolchildren visit the Triceratops. This automated animal once frightened this author, who did not expect movement much less the roar that occurred at the same time when he turned away to read an accompanying exhibit. This occurred when the museum was in the original location at the old school building on Memorial Boulevard.

Before the Virginia Museum of Natural History brought dinosaurs to Martinsville, Sinclair Gasoline brought them for the first time in millions of years. Started in 1916 by Harry Sinclair, the namesake company was once a mainstay on the scene in Martinsville as these images indicate.

David Minter enjoys a cold Coca-Cola from Sinclair's filling station on Chestnut Street in Martinsville in September 1964 as he strides towards the Broad Street Hotel. The McKee Funeral Home is on the right. Notice the S and H Green Stamps sign and the white socks of a dude enjoying a summer day. David, like his father and son, served in the U. S. Army. Below, David and his 1961 Chevy convertible park it for a few moments in front of the Broad Street Hotel.

Recently reopened by the Martinsville Uptown Revitalization Association (MURA) with a grant from the Harvest Foundation, the Rives Theatre on East Church Street shows movies and holds music concerts. With the loss of jobs and industry, these two groups are trying to bring back economic prosperity to the inner city making sites such as the theatre attractive to use and for tourism. Friends of the Rives Theater (FORT) work to revive the theater. Learn more about it at www.martinsvilleuptown.com.

The Chief Tassel Building with a Gulf Station in front and the Astor Café. Below, Eggleston Motors pumped gas from Texaco and below that the first "Service Station" in Martinsville.

This aerial view of downtown Martinsville during the boom days of the textile and chemical industries shows a crowded and vibrant downtown area. DuPont brought a nylon production facility to the area during World War Two and a resulting boom in textiles occurred making Martinsville the "Sweatshirt Capital of the World."

This image of the parking lot on Fayette Street in downtown Martinsville with the City Maintenance Garage in the background reflects the vibrant downtown area after World War Two. Collaborating with the Virginia Foundation for the Humanities, a grassroots effort called the Fayette Area Historical Initiative today includes an African-American History Museum.

     Dr. Dana Owen Baldwin (1881-1972) moved to Martinsville in 1910 as the first African-American physician and set off a business expansion called the Baldwin Block. Credited with businesses such as a brick company, pool hall, dance hall, and café, he served in World War One. His pharmacy shown in this image above was the centerpiece of the block.

The Baldwin Business Center or the "Baldwin Block" was an African-American business district along Fayette Street. Dr. D. O. Baldwin operated St. Mary's hospital above his drug store. Baldwin and his family started Black Fiddler's Conventions, Agricultural Fairs, and the June German Ball recently revived by the Fayette Historical Area Initiative.

  The Fayette Street Museum collects, preserves, and interprets the African American experience in Martinsville and Henry County. Located in a historic landmark, the museum showcases African American history and culture through displays and exhibits. Level one represents more than 100 years of African American history on Fayette Street. The exhibits, "Walking down the street what do you see?" and "Where we were...where are we today?" show 2 miles of road along Fayette Street. While traveling the two-mile stretch, you will see black owned businesses, doctor's offices, retail stores, and other historic buildings. Level two shows black history on the local and national levels. Photo displays of events, educators, doctors, businesses, churches and it's all waiting for your eyes only. One of those who worked tirelessly to get the FAHI off the ground is Linda Dillard, shown below, a great lady with a great enthusiasm for preserving the history of Fayette Street. Learn more about it here www.aaheritageva.org/special%20projects/martinsville.php.

Today, the Baldwin Block is an open area across from the Farmer's Market on one side and one of the main drags of Martinsville, Market Street, a few blocks from the Liberty Fair Mall and the old court house. While some might see a vacant lot, others might imagine a thriving African-American community or a generation before a gunfight along this street, but that is a story for the next page.

Gunfire erupted on May 17, 1886, on Fayette Street in Martinsville, Virginia, in one of the largest gunfights ever recorded on the east coast. This shootout ended with nine shot and eventually three dead including an African-American bystander. It was just five years after Wyatt Earp and the Gunfight at the OK Corral, but that was thousands of miles away in the frontier western town of Tombstone, Arizona. The shooting in Martinsville happened within sight of the Henry County Court House in the middle of a quiet southern town. The fight between the Terrys and the Spencer Brothers, John Dillard Spencer on the left and James Harrison Spencer on the right, shown above has become the thing of myth and legend, but the gunfight occurred and news of it reached as far away as the New York Times.

Whether pride and a question of honor or an imagined romance like Romeo and Juliet between Spencers and Terrys dreamed up in a 1950s romance magazine, the gunfire showed the heightened tensions still prevalent after the War Between the States was just beneath the surface even in Martinsville and within site of the courthouse.

The United States Post Office on Church Street in 1953 Martinsville reflects a slower time with a clock and a newsstand on the corner. Today with the internet slowly strangling the readership, newspapers may soon be history with email, blogs, and websites posing a threat to the postal service.

Thornton's Bakery, located at the corner of Moss and Fayette streets along with their trucks, was a fixture in Henry County delivering bread and cakes. In 2007, forty-two acres of the Fayette Street Historic District and thirteen surrounding streets became part of the Virginia Landmarks Register.

In the days before television and the internet, entertainment often came in the form of public gatherings such as these people gathered on the corner of Church and Main Streets to watch who knows what. The Hamilton Hotel is on the left background and the Setback Building on the right. Below is the laying of the Masonic Temple corner stone at the corner of Bridge and Church Streets on July 1, 1914, with the Hamilton Hotel in the background.

Another event people gathered for was the Floral Parade shown on this page in 1905, which was one of the events centered around the Henry County Fair.

The view above and below is from Kearfott's Drug Store on the courthouse square in Martinsville in the early 1900s.

Inside Kearfott's Drug Store, you could purchase cigars on the left or carbonated water made by Dr. Kearfott himself. Below is a scene from Kearfott's Drug Store in 1903. The two ladies are Mrs. Dillard Ford and Mrs. Mary Semple. (Courtesy of Elva Adams, www.myhenrycounty.com)

The business of downtown Martinsville revolved around commerce and the "long, narrow lobby" of the First National Bank shown above was one of the many places where this movement of people and their funds occurred. On the left is W. E. Mitchell and Irving Ramsey is on the right. Below, the Martinsville Uptown Revitalization Association operates a Farmer's Market each year beginning in May.

Politics was a spectator's sport in the days before television as shown in the image above from 1898. A Republican was giving a speech against Claude A. Swanson, who represented Patrick and Henry Counties and for whom the town of Claudville in Patrick County is named. The downtown was full as Swanson stood nearby at the courthouse speaking. Swanson went on to be Franklin Roosevelt's Secretary of the Navy. Below, is a Saturday morning gathering in downtown Martinsville with several eating melons. On the left are T. N. Barbour's Hardware Store and Jesse Minter's Shoe Shop and lawyer's offices including Plummer Drewry in the frame building in the back right.

Standing on top of the telephone pole in 1903 is Tuck Fontaine, who installed telephones. Notice the three boys below the pole to the left and the people to the right seemingly oblivious to the goings on. On the left is the Setback Building, which housed the law offices of Gravely and Carter with Dentist C. T. Womack's office upstairs. Below, the Williams' Store in the 1940s located in the Knights of the Pythian's building dominated the courthouse square.

Aerial views of downtown Martinsville.

Above on Bridge Street is the "Foundry." Below, looking to the south is the trestle on the Norfolk and Western Railroad with an ice plant operated by A. M. Dudley under the bridge on the left of the railroad bridge. Bottom is the "Dry Bridge" over the Norfolk and Western Railroad on Starling Avenue.

Today, a visit to downtown could include lunch at Arts, Etc. shown here beside the Chief Tassel building. After lunch, a leisurely walk along 0.6-mile the uptown spur of the Smith River Trail, which sits in the former path of the railroad, is a great way to experience downtown Martinsville, Virginia.

Chapter Four
Gone, But Not Forgotten

This aerial image of the DuPont plant from the 1940s in the bend of the Smith River. DuPont was once the largest employer in Martinsville and Henry County. Today, it like many industries is gone, but not forgotten. This 1940 era postcard shows the DuPont Nylon plant in Martinsville. "Horseshoe Bend" on the Smith River is where DuPont built a chemical plant to make Nylon. This postcard shows the white boundary era of postcard design also shows the "Horseshoe Bend of the Smith River" where the DuPont plant was located.

Above, one of the hotels in Martinsville is the Henry Hotel, which opened in 1921. Below are two ladies in front of the Hotel Stevens.

Dr. Tom Simmons sits on a horse in front of Hundley's Livery Stable on the corner of Main Street and Ford Street near the courthouse square.

In the days before chain grocery stores, people canned their fruits and vegetables. The Martinsville Canning Plant shown above was one of the places this occurred.

Above is a Martinsville circa 1899 scene from Gravely Street looking towards Bridge, College, and Broad Streets. Tobacco factories in the photo are the English-Belcher Tobacco factory on the lower right and the large white building in the left center is the Stultz Brothers near the Broad Street Christian Church to the right in the center. Below from October 1874 is one of the earliest views of Martinsville looking southeast at the "Thomas Block" stretching from Bridge to Walnut Streets along Main Street. Businesses are Smith's Hardware, Putzel's General Store, Gregory's Confectionery, Lavinder's Store, and Thomas's Law Office sit where Kearfott's Drug Store later sat.

Above is a 1910 view showing Oak Hall, the home of Colonel Pannill Rucker, a tobacco manufacturer, who built this house about ten years before this image on Church Street. The house was gone seven years later due to fire. Rucker rebuilt the house as a two story home. Rives S. Brown, Sr. finished the house after he purchased it in 1919. Brown sold it to the Pannill Family in 1934. Today, Christ Episcopal Church owns the house and uses it for Sunday school located across the street from the Blue Ridge Regional Library. While the building remains, the time period it represents is gone, but not forgotten.

Dr. Harvey Price, a Martinsville dentist, lived in this home on the corner of Starling Avenue and Spring Street. The stonewall surrounding the home reportedly was from the "burned out" Pannill Home at the present day Christ Episcopal Parish House. (Courtesy of Elva Adams. www.myhenrycounty.com)

Textiles like furniture became a mainstay of the economy of Henry County with facilities such as Pannill Knitting Company located on Cleveland and Water Streets in Martinsville. The Pannills were descended from William Letcher Pannill, the uncle of Civil War General J. E. B. Stuart of neighboring Patrick County. All were descended from William Letcher, the great-grandfather of Stuart, who died during the American Revolution.

Above, William Letcher Pannill is shown kneeling in the front right in a white straw hat with employees of Pannill Knitting Company in 1931. Below. Pannill Knitting Company started producing sweatshirts in the mid-1930s. Orginally, it was the W. A. Brown Company. Mr. Pannill started Virginia Underwear Company with Samuel S. Walker in 1928, which eventually became Bassett-Walker Knitting Company. Pannill started Sale Knitting Company with his son-in-law, E. A. "Mike" Sale, in 1937 and it became Sale Knitting. At one time, Martinsville was the "Sweatshirt Capital of the World."

R. J. Reynolds used the Rucker-Witten-Dudley Tobacco
Building for storage before it was sold to the Martinsville Cotton Mill
organized in 1909, then later became Sale Knitting, Tultex, and is
now The Clocktower at Commonwealth Center owned by Lester
Properties, which now occupies this building 1.1 million square foot
facility that has seen the history of Martinsville.

This image above shows the Rucker-Witten Tobacco Factory under construction located near Liberty Fair Mall. Later sold to R. J. Reynolds Tobacco for storage, it became the Martinsville Cotton Mill, Sale Knitting, Tultex, and now the Commonwealth Center. It reflects the tobacco and textile industries now gone that once dominated the area's economy. Below are the officers in 1904. Front row are C. B. Keesee, B. A. Reeves, Col. Pannill Rucker, A. D. Witten, and Gabe Holmes. Middle row are Ralph Faulkner, Mr. Carr, unidentified youngster, Thomas J. Jones, John Simmons, Jim Patterson and Jack Rudd. On the back row are J. E. Howard, Capt. R. M. Morgan, John S. Williams, H. D. Vickers, Henry Harity, Fred Williams, G. M. Andes, and D. H. Pannill.

This image of the Lee Telephone Company Building located on Church Street in Martinsville reflects a time when local entrepreneurs started utilities. Work began each Monday with a Sunday school and a church service for all employees except the operators who kept the switchboard. Below is the Piedmont Creamery Company.

This image is of Jobbers Pants Factory located on Fayette and Market Streets in Martinsville. Jobbers, founded in 1933, was one of many textile manufacturing companies that drove the region's economy with Bassett-Walker, Pannill Knitting, Sale, and Tultex being some of the manufacturers in Henry County that produced mainly sweatpants and cotton t-shirts. Today, most of these factories stand empty. The loss of jobs and economic base is making the region rethink economic development. Below is Standard Garments, a division of Jobbers Pants Company.

First called the Martinsville Christian Institute and founded in 1900 by the Fayette Street Christian Church, the Henry County Training School's eighteen room Smith Hall rose in 1906. Before it burned in the 1940s, the school provided education to African-American students. Until integration, Albert Harris High School continued this work beginning in 1948.

Planter's Warehouse was another of the plethora of tobacco operations in Martinsville where you could hear auctioneers in their "sing-song" pricing the crop brought to market by farmers sometimes as far away as Danville.

Martinsville School, built in 1904 above, took the place of Ruffner Institute, shown at the bottom. Ruffner was the first school in Martinsville established in 1877. L. Starling Thomas donated land for it on the corner of Brown Street and Cleveland Avenue. Originally all grades held classes here, but it later became Central Grammar School.

Mr. and Mrs. E. H. Brewer operated the Picnic Tavern, where the slogan was "Try your own meal here." One mile south of Martinsville on Route 220 south, you could get a BBQ sandwich for a dime along with "All Kinds of Sandwiches." Below is the Townes Building, the home of Henry County Furniture, which burned in 1951.

Destroyed by the same fire mentioned on the preceding page in 1951, the Banner Warehouse operated by E. J. Davis for more than forty years selling tobacco.

Athol, the home built by Judge Stafford Gorman Whittle, sat on Church Street above and below from the porch of the home. Judge Whittle and his son, Kennon C. Whittle, served on the Virginia Supreme Court.

Chatmoss, built as a wedding present for Alcie Hairston when she married Sam Harden in the 1800s was one of the many Hairston homes regionally. A fire destroyed the house in 1928 and an English country house replaced it, but it burned too. Today, Chatmoss is a private country club east of Martinsville. Below is the entrance hall to Chatmoss, one of the many palatial homes in Henry County and the surrounding area that was home to the Hairstons.

Chapter Five
Play Ball

     Eugene Copeland, when not kicking footballs at Martinsville High School, worked at Faggs Drug Store. He carpooled from Fieldale to play football. Called "the girls' pet" or the "soda jerker," he graduated in 1929. His interest in girls ended one day when as if in a scene from "It's a Wonderful Life," his future wife, Mary Hurd, walked in the drug store.

Sonny Wade of Martinsville High School was Virginia College player of the year three times playing at Emory and Henry College 1966-68. Drafted by the Philadelphia Eagles, Wade chose to play for the Montreal Allouttes of the Canadian Football League leading them to three championships and the same number of Most Valuable Player awards.

These are the 1966 Industrial Softball Champions of Martinsville from DuPont. The front row includes John Pulliam, Buford Campbell, Scott White, Jimmy Doyle, Wendell Hubbard, and Dave Ehly. The back row includes Jimmy Caldwell, Daryl Grindstaff, Curtis Tilley, Roger Scott, and Teddy Compton. DuPont won championships in baseball, basketball, and bowling.

Before the days of integration, DuPont sponsored separate teams for their African-American employees. This baseball team from the 1950s included George Reed, James Naylon, Steve Wingfield, and Robert Spencer on the front row. The second row included Johnny Burnette, Russell Wingfield, James Draper, George Strickland, and James Redd. The third row includes James Ellis, Joe Taylor, Lee Patterson, Llewellyn Moyer, and John Hylton.

Baseball player Bill Curlee played on DuPont and Martinsville teams. Almost forgotten now was the Bi-State League formed in 1934 that included ten teams from Virginia and North Carolina including the Fieldale Virginians who played until 1942. The Bassett Furnituremakers won the title four times including three in a row from 1936-38.

Baseball was and still is popular in Martinsville. Above are the Martinsville-Henry County All Stars of 1958. Below a team from the 1934 Brown Street Field. Front row are Jimmy Sanders, Al Casey, Tom Noval, Norman Small, Joe Ariola, Nick Urezetti and Delos Jones. Back row are Al Sherer, Joe Concannon, Al Krupski, Lee Putman, Sam Narron, Mutt Miller, Jesus Miralles, and co-owners Fred Woodson, Jr. and James R. English. (Courtesy of Elva Adams, www.myhenrycounty.com)

Football, including state championships, is part of the
Martinsville High School history. Above is the football team from
1920. Front row are Robert Ferguson, Tilman Hurd, Booker Carter,
Vernon English, W. T. Turner, and Herman Slaydon. Middle row are
John B. Sparrow, John Matthews, Chauncey Drewry, Clyde Byrd,
Pete Carter, Tom Barbour, and Julian Kester. Back row are Howard
Whitlow, Coach Wilbur Gregory, Milton Andes, Jack Jackson, John
M. Richardson, Alonza Hedgecock, Dick Pulliam and John A.
Ramsey, manager. The Philadelphia Eagles drafted Carl Hairston
shown below in 1976 from Maryland-Eastern Shore. He played in
Super Bowl XV against the Oakland Raiders. He played fifteen
seasons in the NFL including stops in Cleveland and Arizona. He
coached professional football beginning in 1991 mainly with the
Kansas City Chiefs, but also the St. Louis Rams and Green Bay
Packers.

Shawn Moore played at Martinsville High School before going on to play at the University of Virginia, where he won a share of the ACC Championship in 1989. He played in the NFL and Canadian Football League from 1991-95. He recently coached at St. Albans School in Washington, D. C. before leaving to join the staff at his alma mater under new coach Mike London in 2010.

The Martin brothers of Martinsville, Cam and Orion, played high school football at Danville's George Washington High School before having stellar careers at Virginia Tech in the first decade of the twenty-first century. They are part of the dynasty Frank Beamer brought to Blacksburg dominating the Big East and now the ACC and especially their neighbors to the north in Charlottesville.

Lou Whitaker, known as "Sweet Lou," played second base for the Detroit Tigers from 1977 until 1995. He was born in Brooklyn and raised in Martinsville. He won three Golden Gloves and was in five All Star Games. He participated in more double plays than anyone in Tigers history with 1,527. He was the 1978 American League Rookie of the Year and played on the 1984 World Series Champion Tigers team.

Playing for Granny's Donuts are Kelvin Craigshead, Steve Slusher, Charles Bird, Ron Matthews, Steve Shough, James Kidd, Shawn Swanson, Eddie Cassady, Gary Smith, Carter Martin, and others.

Not all football players from Martinsville played at UVA or Virginia Tech. Delvin Joyce played at James Madison University before playing two years with the New York Football Giants. Born in Martinsville, Joyce was a kickoff and punt return specialist.

Rahib Abdullah, born in Martinsville in 1975, grew up in New Jersey, and played college football at Lehigh University. He ran for over 3,500 yards in college. He played in the NFL for the Tampa Bay Buccaneers, Chicago Bears, and the Super Bowl XXXIX Champion New England Patriots in February 2005.

Chapter Six
Court House Square

The Henry County Courthouse shown above looking up Bridge Street from Church Street in 1905 and below in 2010. Virginia formed the county in 1776 from Pittsylvania County for its first Governor Patrick Henry, who later moved to the area. George Hairston donated the land this structure sits on today. This 1929 structure is the third courthouse on the site. The grounds on the front lawn honor the service of those from Henry County in the armed services. The county courts and related government offices moved to a new facility abandoning the structure.

From the roof of a nearby building, possibly People's Bank, the Henry County Court House in the 1930s was the seat of government beginning from 1793 and in need of some tree and shrub trimming. In 2010, efforts are underway to restore the building and use it for meeting space and a museum under the auspices of the Martinsville-Henry County Historical Society.

Martinsville Police Officer David Taft Stanford served the city for thirty-four years beginning in 1936. Known for saying, "Hi, fella. Just take it easy." whether greeting you or arresting you, he was a fixture around town. Shown here in front of the courthouse, Stanford was a veteran of World War Two, a member of the First Baptist Church, American Legion, and Veterans of Foreign Wars. He married Elizabeth Wells and had two children, a son and a daughter. In September 1961, a car accident took the lives of his children and a daughter-in-law leaving his two grandchildren orphans.

The courthouse from the early 1920s and the cover for this book. Notice the steps leading up to the second floor that no longer are part of the building. The Mildred Lee Chapter of the United Daughters of the Confederacy erected the Confederate Monument on the right in 1901.

Moon over Martinsville is one of the four postcards of the courthouse.

Uptown Martinsville about 1930. Note Twin City Grocery at the bottom of the hill, Globmans and Kolodnys stores and a small sign for Goldberg's. (Courtesy of Elva Adams, www.myhenrycounty.com) Below is Kearfott's Drug Store on the right in this image of the courthouse square looking up Main Street.

This 1941 image above of the courthouse square in downtown Martinsville shows Globman's Department Store, the A and P Super Market and the Townes Building, the "Home of Better Furniture." A cannon on the left shows the location of the Henry County Courthouse. The Globman family was part of a vibrant Jewish community in town. Below, a traffic jam in the 1930s ushered in the era of the automobile.

A high diver in 1905 takes a leap of faith in front of the courthouse. The courthouse square was a focal point for the downtown area in Martinsville whether it was special events such as this or the circus elephants seen on other pages. Mainly, the area around the courthouse was for legal and commercial business in a time when travel was via literal horsepower and not combustible engines.

The front lawn of the courthouse is and remains a place to remember those who made sacrifice to the growing nation. One of those receiving such recognition is Brigadier General Joseph Martin, who gave Martinsville its name. His resting place is near his last home in eastern Henry County along Leatherwood Creek, but this marker recognizes his service to the nation.

A marker to the war dead of Henry County and Martinsville is opposite this marker and a marker to the Confederate dead from the War Between the States sits near Martin's marker.

The Virginia Historical Highway marker denotes Martin, Patrick Henry and incorrectly states that General Stoneman, who did not visit Martinsville, was headed to meet General Sherman. No such meeting occurred or was planned. Stoneman raided towards Salisbury, North Carolina, while Sherman was further east near Durham, North Carolina.

In 1908, an unknown driver is carrying Nora Weisiger, Hunter Pannill, John Hamilton, Laura and Hattie Barrett for a ride by the courthouse. Two eras passing as the day of the ox driven cart meets the automobile in front of the courthouse.

A circus mural recently painted on the wall of the New College Institute on Main Street in uptown Martinsville was inspired by a 1920s-era photograph of elephants walking past the old Henry County courthouse in uptown Martinsville as part of a visiting circus. A local artist, John Stiles, turned that photograph into the mural design. The outline of his original design was transferred to the wall by Jeff Magnum of North Carolina, and hand-painted by Jessie Ward and other local artists.

A fire nearly destroyed the Watt Hairston Building, home of the Knights of the Pythians, then, and today on the west side of the courthouse square.

In the 1920s, Congressman Claude Swanson got cannons for the Martinsville Henry County Courthouse from Fort McHenry, Maryland, where the words for the Star Spangled Banner were penned by Francis Scott Key during the War of 1812. One tradition says that the only problem was when they arrived there was no way to get them from the train tracks to their present resting site due to their enormous weight. Horses could not do the job, but when a circus came to town the animals pulled the cannons to the courthouse. A great story, but some say not true.

The courthouse dates back to 1824, but was renovated and enlarged in 1929. Today, efforts are underway to transfer ownership to the Martinsville Henry County Historical Society to turn the building into a museum and meeting facility as part of efforts to revitalize the area around the square including the New College Institute.

During the term of Attorney Deborah Hall as President of the Martinsville-Henry County Historical Society the rear dilapidated annex of the courthouse was torn down to improve the appearance of the courthouse and to make way for future renovations. Also, Hall started the process to get the Save A Treasure grant for the courthouse.

Above, displaying artifacts from his large collection of historical artifacts is Doug Stegall at the courthouse in April 2010. Below, the view from the back of the courthouse shows the preservation of history with the rail trail, the efforts to bring new business in the former Tultex building and the new hospital in the distance reflecting the past, present, and the future of Martinsville.

Above, Members of the Stuart-Hairston Sons of Confederate Veterans Camp #515 "The Henry Guards" remember their ancestors in the War Between the States at an event at the courthouse that included a memorial service in April 2010.

The courthouse is the center of hopes to revitalize downtown. Below the history still lives around the building while the sacrifice of those from Martinsville and Henry County who gave all the wars of the United and Confederate States of America is remembered in the monument. The Watt Hairston Building, former home of the Knights of the Pythians sits in the background.

Chapter Seven
Extraordinary Folks

This image circa 1963 shows Clearview Elementary School teacher Beverly Lipford Yeager in Martinsville. The city operates a separate school system from Henry County that includes Clearview Early Educational Center, Patrick Henry and Albert Harris Elementary Schools, Martinsville Middle School and Martinsville High School. Albert Harris was an African-American Methodist Minister, who started a school for Black children.

Beverly single handedly produced over fifty articles for the Henry County Heritage Book edited by this author in 2009-2010. Her dedication to the effort earned her a special place in the hearts of those who worked on the book and in this chapter as one of the extraordinary folks of Martinsville, Virginia. (Courtesy of Beverly Yeager.)

From Stonehenge in England above to the stage of the Grand Ole Opry in Nashville below, Josh Shilling's musical talent has carried him from far from home in Henry County. He never forgets where he came from, whether singing the National Anthem with his band Mountain Heart at the Martinsville Speedway or opening for Lynyrd Skynyrd, Josh has come a long way since he began playing piano at age seven. (Courtesy of Josh Shilling.)

Two members of the Lester Family of Martinsville and Henry County are above, George Tilden "Cap'n Til" Lester, and his nephew, Ralph Lester, below. Founder of the Lester Lumber Company, "Cap'n Til" is known for the Liberty Heights Swimming Pool and the "Wedding Cake House." Ralph Lester, a pioneer in modular housing is known for his support of education and in his ninth decade is still involved in his community.

The officers of the Virginia Lambda Chapter of Beta Sigma Phi are Miss Judy Harris, Mrs. Marion Hargrove, Mrs. Joseph Richardson, Miss Beverly Lipford, now Yeager, and Miss Patsy Penn. Below, Beverly Lipford Yeager as part of the Clearview School faculty in 1965 along with Ruth Ross, Irene Brogan, Juanita Hewitt, Pat Martin, Virginia Draper, Louise Edwards, Mrs. A. L. Parr Hill, Evelyn Walton, Mina Kornegay, David Chittum, Jean Ross, Frieda Stevenson, Betty Goins, Gwen Bow, Janie Garraghty, Harold Bumberledge, and Nancy White.

Rives S. Brown, Sr., the son of Tarleton Brown, lost his parents at an early age and found himself in the care of his uncle Henry Clay Lester and aunt Lucy Brown Lester. Brown was responsible for the development of the Lanier Farm area and the residential community along Mulberry in Martinsville. His son continued his business and a real estate firm still bears his name. (Courtesy of Elva Adams, www.myhenrycounty.com)

The DuPont Guard Force was security for the Martinsville nylon manufacturing facility. E. I. du Pont de Nemours and Company came from France to manufacture gunpowder in 1802 along Brandywine Creek in Delaware. By the time it came to Henry County, nylon was the commodity and its importance made Martinsville a "strategic bombing" site during the Cold War.

Alexander D. Goode (1911-1943) was the son of a Jewish Rabbi who lived for a time in Martinsville. He gave his life with three other chaplains in the U. S. Army when the USAT Dorchester sank during World War Two. Grace Baptist Church in Philadelphia honors the chaplains with a stained glass window dedicated in 1951 by President Truman. Below are members of Company H, 29th Division during World War Two.

Linda and Steve Cole of Martinsville, a carpenter and customer service supervisor, appeared on CBS television's Amazing Race show in 2008. Married seventeen years, they have children from previous marriages. While they did not win the race, they are just some of the "Amazing" people from Martinsville.

Sam Hairston sitting in the brown ladder back chair on display at the Bassett Historical Center that his great-grandfather John Burgess, a slave on the farm of John Henry Burgess, passed down through his family. (Courtesy of the Martinsville Bulletin.)

"Samuel Blankenship and Lawrence McAuley were World War II veterans who were working for the American Optical Company when they decided to open their own company which they named "Martinsville Optical." Martinsville Optical opened November 2, 1951, on 13 Bridge Street, in Martinsville Virginia, the only independent retail optical company in the area. There were no additional employees until 1966, when Jerry Wimmer was hired as an optician. In 1971, Mr. Blankenship, joined the company. Martinsville Optical then moved to its present location on 749 East Church Street. Martinsville Optical is now operated by James E. Blankenship and has four employees, one office manager, and three opticians." (Courtesy of Anne White.)

Brevet Brigadier General William Jackson Palmer led a brigade of George Stoneman's men through Martinsville leaving for Danbury, North Carolina, on April 9, 1865, the day Robert E. Lee surrenderd at Appomattox Court House ending the Civil War in Virginia. Major General George Stoneman of New York shown below, a roommate of Thomas J. "Stonewall" Jackson at West Point in the fabled class of 1846, did not visit Henry County, but was with the main body of his 4,000 man cavalry in Patrick County. Stoneman later became Governor of California.

Frank Stringfellow served J. E. B. Stuart and John Mosby as a scout in northern Virginia during the War Between the States. He came to Martinsville in the 1890s to serve as Rector for Christ Episcopal Church.

Dr. Morton E. Hundley, who practiced medicine in Martinsville is shown feeding pigeons in Europe on his third honeymoon. He attended the Medical College of Virginia and Johns Hopkins Medical School. He died of a heart attack on January 2, 1928, in Switzerland. He started the Lucy Lester Hospital named for his second wife on Church Street in Martinsville.

Cassie Gravely, who died in 1967 at age 93, wrote the official salute to the Virginia flag, which read, "I salute the Flag of Virginia with reverence and patriotic devotion to the 'Mother of States and Statesmen' which it presents the 'Old Dominion' where Liberty and Independence were born." Governor Thomas Stanley of Henry County signed the salute into law in 1954.

With chickens, ducks, dogs, and children are Dr. Henry M. Drewry and his wife Flora at their home on the corner of Church and Cleveland Streets in Martinsville. Drewry-Mason school gets its name partly from the doctor. Notice the laundry drying on the rope and ivy growing along the side of the house. (Courtesy of John Bing.)

Martinsville Convalescent Center was the first nursing home in Henry County as this image of a Christmas party shows. Today modern facilities such as King's Grant on the land once owned by the Hairston Family continue nursing and retirement facilities for the elderly providing a good quality of life. (Courtesy of Deborah Hodges.)

This image is of Jesse Frith working with T29 nylon on the second floor of the DuPont plant in Martinsville. For safety purposes, he wears safety glasses, long sleeves, and no jewelry. The DuPont website says, "Nylon was the world's first true synthetic textile fiber. It now is found in hundreds of applications from carpets to clothing to luggage to automobile parts." Beginning in 1941, the company began operations and continued until 1998 when nylon manufacturing ceased, DuPont was an important part of the Henry County economy. Today the name DuPont returns twice a year on the NASCAR racecar of Jeff Gordon #24 at the Martinsville Speedway. (Courtesy of Joan Frith.)

This image from October 1962 shows the Magnificent Seven playing three nights, Thursday through Saturday starting at 7:30 p.m. at the Collinsville Center. The seven are Ronnie Mitchell, Mike Clay, Gary Wayne Hill, Morgan Armstrong, Leon Stone, and David Arnold. Sitting in the middle is the "mascot" and future attorney and Virginia Delegate Ward Armstrong.

The Martinsville Concert Band in 1921 are front row, left to right John Nuckols, W. W. Clingenpeel, Milton Andes, Booker Carter, John Moore, William Stultz, Starling E. Shumate, Ernest C. Stultz, John Letcher English, Jr., and J. A. Stultz. Second row are, A. C. Drewry, Tillman Hurd, P. Dillard Smith, Decatur Hutchinson, Russell Slaydon, W. H. Harris, J. Leonard Stultz, and Claude Slaydon.

This Henry County Democratic Party meeting in Martinsville includes among others from left to right; Gold Prillaman, Arthur Horsely, S. E. Moran, John Philpott, Lafayette Prillaman, J. L. Racey, James Franklin, Stover Terry, Clyde Fentress, Branch K. Rives, J. W. Vipperman, seated at the left of the table wearing a pair argyle socks is Lowell Young. (Courtesy of Vickie Stone Helmstutler.)

This 1956 image shows Julian Hurst, the first City Manager of Martinsville, who later went to Roanoke, Virginia, and Principal R. T. Anderson of East Martinsville School. Immediately to Hurst's right is Thomas T. Hodge, Jr. With schools still segregated and two years after the 1954 Brown Supreme Court decision, this group came together as part of the fire safety program of the Martinsville Fire Department. (Courtesy of Jerry Brock.)

Many famous visitors came to Martinsville including Henry Ford above and Thomas Edison below standing in the long coat and beret with his son Charles at the Hamilton Hotel in 1906. Ford came through in 1910 on his way to Florida carrying his wife and Harvey Firestone.

On August 20, 2008, Democratic Presidential candidate U.S. Senator Barack Obama of Illinois and former Virginia Governor Mark R. Warner campaigned together at the Patrick Henry Community College and Arrington Motor Sports in Martinsville, Virginia. Both won election as President and Senator, respectively.

Thomas Granville Burch began as a farmer in Dyer's Store and then moved his tobacco business to Martinsville. He began a political career as mayor until elected to the U. S. House of Representatives in 1930. He served until he took the U. S. Senate seat of the recently deceased Carter Glass.

Still another dinosaur in Martinsville, but this is covered in ice cream. For any author the place to be in Martinsville is the Binding Time Café from this author to John Grisham shown with Bonnie and John Hale, Congressman Tom Perriello, and Kelsey Cooper in July 2008. Even a dinosaur donated by Bud Thomas with ice cream that the café sells hangs out at the Binding Time. (Courtesy of Bonnie and John Hale, www.binding-time.com)

William Letcher Pannill in 1932 was a nephew of Confederate Major General James Ewell Brown Stuart. Pannill Knitting Company was one of the many major textile manufacturers in Martinsville.

William Roscoe Reynolds was born in Martinsville in 1942. He attended Duke and then Washington and Lee University Law School. He represented Henry County in the Virginia House of Delegates from 1986 until 1997. He moved to the Virginia Senate representing the 20th district.

In 1898, the Choral Club gave an Old Folks Concert. First row are Mary Williams, Maggie Smith, Mary Lavinder, and Jennie Brown. Second row are Helen Dillard Morris, Dr. Will Shackelford, Alice Gravely, Dr. Arthur Rowbothan, Hassie Fuller, and Charles Maury. Back row are P. T. Morris, Mrs. Charles Maury, Annie Matthews, Reverend Hugh Smith, Annette Fuller and Frances Fishburn.

Below, Magdalen Hsu-Li, born to Chinese immigrants in Martinsville, writes and produces her own music. Described as a blend of alternative rock, pop, folk, and jazz, her musical career began playing piano at age 8. She has three albums: Fire, Evolution, and Smashing the Ceiling. She paints, writes poetry, and calls herself a cultural activist.

The Palace Barber Shop around 1920 on Bridge Street. Mr. W. H. Hairston on the right started cutting hair on a tree stump in his yard. Below, Martinsville Mayor G. A. Brown served for twenty-one years beginning in 1915. Described as "very popular," he even directed traffic.

Above the Penn brothers, John, William, Joseph, and Thomas Green fought in the War Between the States. Their home Aurora, "The Pink House," is just over the line in Patrick County. Roberto Sanchez came to Martinsville via northern Virginia from El Salvador. He owns the Penn home Aurora in neighboring Patrick County and Rania's Restaurant on the corner of Main and Lester streets with his uncle, Herbert Alvado. Roberto, his wife, Vilma and daughters, Erica, Iliana and Vanessa live in "The Pink House" that is on Virginia and National Registers of Historic Places.

John Redd Smith, Sr. above with his horse Christmas and on the right below. The building behind him with the vines was the home of the Martinsville Herald on the corner of Walnut and Church streets. Below right is Sallie Reamey Pannill Smith, John's wife, the daughter of Eliza Reamey and Edmund J. Pannill. Bottom is their son, John Redd Smith, Jr. celebrating his 85th year in 2010.

Major John Redd, above right, built Belleview in 1783. It was the ancestral home of many prominent people of Martinsville and Henry County including Judge Kennon C. Whittle. It is one of the few sites in the county denoted with a Virginia Historical Highway Marker shown above left.

Judge Stafford Gorman Whittle, his wife Ruth Staples Drewry, and family around 1910. Whittle practiced law in Martinsville beginning in 1871 and became a judge ten years later. Elected to the Virginia Supreme Court of Appeals in 1901, he served there until 1919. He was associated with Christ Episcopal Church and lived in Martinsville until his death in 1931. His father was William Conway Whittle, who served in both the United States and Confederate Navies.

His son, Kennon C. Whittle (1891-1967), is on the far right on the front row. Born in Martinsville and educated at Washington and Lee, Kennon became a circuit court judge and in 1951 followed his father to the Supreme Court of Appeals serving until 1965. Before that he was the judge on the "Martinsville Seven" case, where a jury convicted the seven men accused of raping a woman in January 1949. The Commonwealth of Virginia executed the men Booker T. Millner, Frank Hairston, Jr., Howard Lee Hairston, Joe Henry Hampton, John Claybon Taylor, Francis Descales Grayson, and James Luther Hairston, in 1951.

Stephen Mark Rainey is a writer, primarily of dark fantasy/horror fiction. He grew up in Martinsville, near Lake Lanier, and graduated from Martinsville High School in 1977. He attended Ferrum College for two years and then transferred to the University of Georgia. During the 1980s, he lived in Chicago for several years before returning south and settling in Greensboro, North Carolina. He still maintains a close connection with friends and family in Martinsville.

Much of Mark's writing is set in a fictionalized version of Martinsville. His bibliography includes several novels (*Balak, The Lebo Coven, Blue Devil Island, The Nightmare Frontier, Dark Shadows: Dreams of the Dark* [with Elizabeth Massie]), over 90 published short stories, and five short-story collections. He has edited several anthologies of horror stories and for ten years (1987–1997) edited the award-winning *Deathrealm* magazine. He currently writes scripts for audio dramas produced by Big Finish (UK), based on the *Dark Shadows* TV series (1966–1971), which include cast members from the original ABC-TV series. Mark's website is www.stephenmarkrainey.com.

Above is J. Frank Wilson, known as "Mr. Fieldale," who served as Mayor of Martinsville and Chairman of the Henry County Board of Supervisors. Today, J. Frank Wilson Park honors his service. Below is Mayor Nick Prillaman, first elected in 1947. He oversaw the government changed to the City Manager form making him the last mayor to actually head the government. He ran unsuccessfully for Lt. Governor in 1949.

      The story of Sam Lion is a 150-year-old narrative of brutally and deadly revenge between a slave and his overseer. There are several versions of the tale, which have assured and measured him immortality by having a Martinsville street named, Sam Lions Trail, in Forest Park named for him. Around the mid 1800s, it was a 1050-acre tract belonging to the Hairstons. The story goes that Sam Lion, the son of an African chieftain, was brought to this country, and bought by one of the Hairstons. As the slaves started to walk from the auction stand, the hot, tired Prince slipped and almost fell. "Watch it there, Sam." From then on the Prince was known as Sam. Legend has it that the slave acquired his last name because he acted noble and with courage as a Lion. Tradition holds that the Hairstons divided their land into sections and sent Sam Lion and other slaves to clear one area. Instead of climbing all the hills to get to work, Sam Lion cleared a path around them. Red Tupper, the overseer, beat his slaves for little reason. One day he beat Sam Lion the slave, knowing little English, responded, "If you beat again, I kill." Tupper merely laughed. But the next day Lion stopped to pick up a chain he had dropped, Tupper hit him with a whip. Lion reportedly straightened up and roared. "Didn't believe?" The slave then picked up his axe, swung it, and killed his overseer. Lion fled into the nearby woods and for three years, he lived off the land, sleeping in caves and watching for signs of anyone searching for him. In time, the story holds searchers found Lion sleeping in a cave. Taken to jail, a court tried and found him guilty of murder. Authorities hung Sam in the public square.

Henry Clay Lester was born on February 25, 1838. He married Lucy Clark Brown, age 16, on August 10, 1871. Henry Clay Lester left his own remarkable story as businessman and leader. This Lester comes down to us as a man of "frail physique," who hired an "Irishman" for $800 to serve as a substitute for him during the Civil War. Lester said he was "not interested in fighting, but interested in enterprise." Henry began a tobacco business after the War Between the States. Henry had the "Midas Touch" with everything he touched in business turning to gold. Lester diversified his business interests by being a merchant, a farmer with the Lanier Farms, handling livestock, and milling with the Lester Livestock and Grain Company, but most of all as a "tobacconist." After moving to Martinsville, H. C. Lester lived there for over twenty-six years. He constructed over 100 buildings along with three flourmills and three saw mills in Henry County. He joined the Christian Church in Martinsville in 1884 and ten years later constructed a building at his own expense for the Broad Street Christian Church. He built the Broad Street Hotel, which his wife converted to a hospital, the Lucy Lester Hospital. H. C. Lester not only had his own businesses, but was involved in many other regional enterprises serving as a President of Farmers Bank of Martinsville, Vice-President of the First National Bank of Martinsville when the former merged with the latter, Director of Virginia and North Carolina Construction and President and Director of the Danville and New River Railroad. Henry Clay Lester lived until September 18, 1913. The day of his funeral all the businesses in Martinsville closed as a sign of respect.

Chapter Eight
All Aboard

This image shows a southbound train at the Norfolk and Western Railroad Station circa 1910 on Broad Street in Martinsville. This railroad came in 1892 along with the Danville and Western, the "Dick and Willie," which came to the city in 1881. Railroads brought the telegraph, electricity, and the telephone following the route of the tracks along with passengers, mail and freight service. (Courtesy of Kenney Kirkman.)

This image taken from the caboose of a northbound freight train by Kenney Kirkman on the Norfolk and Western Railroad in 1976 shows the Broad Street Station at Martinsville. The manufacturing plant of American Furniture is in the background. Fire destroyed the factory in 1995 and the railroad station in 1978. (Courtesy of Kenney Kirkman.)

Postcards of the image from 1910 above of the Norfolk and Western Station in Martinsville. Below is a postcard of the Danville and Western or "Dick and Willie" Railway passenger station in uptown Martinsville at the corner of Franklin and Depot Streets, which was torn down after World War II.

This image shows the Norfolk and Western Railway Station burning in Martinsville in spite of the best efforts of the Martinsville Fire Department on September 9, 1978. (Courtesy of Jerry Brock.) Below, is an early 1900s view looking south of Martinsville's Norfolk and Western Railway Station on Broad Street.

Above is an early view of a doubleheaded Norfolk and Western Railroad freight train northbound at Martinsville led by two steam locomotives in the vicinity of Starling Avenue. Below is an image showing the Danville and Western, the "Dick and Willie," the other railroad that came into Martinsville in the late 1800s. Chartered in 1873 as a narrow gauge railroad, the D and W was the first railroad to come to Martinsville in 1882. Two years later the line ran from Stuart to Danville and continued for the next sixty years.

Above, a Danville and Western Railroad, the "Dick and Willie" and crew beside a passenger train after conversion to standard gauge (4 feet eight and one-half inches.) Originally, called the Danville and New River Railroad it was a narrow gauge (3 feet between the rails.) Below, the modern line of the Norfolk Southern, Engine 1331 leads a northbound train near Martinsville along the former Norfolk and Western Railway in 1989. This line still runs from Winston-Salem, North Carolina, to Roanoke, Virginia, and through Martinsville seven days a week since starting in 1891.

Beginning as the Roanoke and Southern, the railroad became the Norfolk and Western and eventually Norfolk Southern, the line was known as the "Punkin Vine" due to the many curves along the route. Above is a northbound Norfolk and Western Railway passenger train arriving at Martinsville in the early 1950s. American Furniture Company is in the background. Below, is not a scene from "The Wild Wild West" television show from the 1960s, but is the "Dick and Willie" from a time long ago when people answered the call "All Aboard" to travel to and from Martinsville.

Chapter Nine
Just Racing

Martinsville Speedway came from the mind of H. Clay Earles, shown below, who started the Martinsville Speedway in 1949. It now operated as a dirt track with seats for 750 until 1955 when paved. The track holds two NASCAR races each year contributing significant economic impact in the region with over 60,000 attending each race.

This 1939 Ford Coupe is "loaded for business." The business of delivering illicit liquor tax free or "Bootlegging." The term originates from hiding a flask of illegal alcohol in a boot covered by a pant leg. Modern car racing and many of the early drivers of NASCAR got their start running liquor by the light of the moon giving us the term "moonshine." (Courtesy of Harold Smith.) Below, an aerial view of the Martinsville Speedway in the 1970s.

"The King" of NASCAR, Richard Petty #43 Richard Petty dominated Martinsville winning the most races with fifteen wins at the half-mile track south of Martinsville. He holds the records for most top fives, top tens, and most starts with 67 at the track.

Above, the stock car series ran for the Winston Cup when R. J. Reynolds sponsored NASCAR and is now the Sprint Cup. Bobby Allison in the car owned by Bassett Virginia's own "Perk" Brown at the Martinsville Speedway in 1950s. Martinsville was one of the first paved racetracks. Many local drivers and NASCAR drivers enjoyed running at the racetrack in other classes of cars as they still do at Oak Level and other dirt tracks in the area. (Courtesy of Harold Smith.)

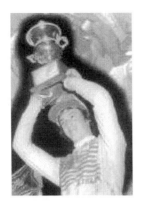

Not all racing from Martinsville and Henry County is
NASCAR. David Bailey, a graduate of the Carlisle School in Henry
County, was a ten time World Motor Cross and ten time National
Champion. Paralyzed from the waist down in 1987, Bailey works as
an ESPN commentator on motorcycle racing and speaks for the Full
Circle Foundation that works to find assistance for those with and to
find a cure for spinal cord injuries.

Martinsville Speedway is the shortest track on the Sprint Cup
Series in 2010 at just over one half mile with 12 degree banking. The
concrete track received an asphalt cover in 2004. The first NASCAR
race occurred in 1948 and each year in March and October fans return
to the track to continue a tradition over sixty years old at this writing.

Not everyone who raced at Martinsville drove Stock Cars in the NASCAR Winston Cup and now Nextel Series. Jim Lambert, Anthony Terry, and Bernie Epperson of Ararat, Virginia, raced at Martinsville in 1970s and 1980s.

Blane Atkins began racing go-carts at age ten and won 20 of the first 30 races he participated in. At the wise age of 15, he ran Allison Legacy in Virginia, North and South Carolina. (Courtesy of Blane Atkins.)

Buddy Arrington raced in NASCAR's Grand National and Winston Cup series. Although he never won a race he finished in the top ten in points twice and was second all time with 567 starts without a win. He was the last driver to run a Chrysler vehicle and completed 147,899 laps.

This image from October 29, 1909, looking west on Church Street shows a car racing in the Glidden Tour that went from New York City to Atlanta, Georgia, along the "National Highway." Eight "gas buggies" and twenty people came through Martinsville trying to prove that automobiles were reliable. Following are images of racing in Martinsville over the years.

Martinsville Speedway being a short track is a place where the term "Just Racin" echoes due to the large number of wrecks and lower speeds requires more driving tactics and sometimes that involves cars making contact is ways that excite the race fans, but are not easy on the cars, drivers, crews and their owners, but, Hey, that is just racin.

Martinsville Speedway hosts the Camping World Truck Series, Whelen Modified Tour, which is held on Labor Day weekend under the lights, and Late Model races along with the NASCAR races each year. Winners receive a "longcase clock" to reflect the furniture business in and around Martinsville.

In 2004, the France Family's (International Speedway Corporation) purchased the track from the Earles family for $192 million dollars. In recent years, plans to expand the seating capacity by 20,000 people resulted in Norfolk Southern Railroad moving the tracks near the speedway 200 feet further away. (Preceding photos courtesy of Jerry Brock.)

Chapter Ten
A River Runs Through It

"Several hundred years before the first Europeans arrived on the shores of what is now Virginia, the Smith River basin was a rich, fertile valley, a natural resource supporting an abundance of wildlife in its streams and forest, sustaining the first humans on our shores. Evidence of these first Americans can still be seen in the form of ancient fish weirs located in the Smith River representing some of the oldest man-made structures in Henry County.

Native American fish dams (weirs) are located along several sections of the Smith River through Henry County but perhaps the most famous is the Martinsville Fish Dam, owned by the Patrick-Henry Chapter of the Archeological Society of Virginia and listed in the National Register of Historic Places. Just downstream from the Route 966 Bridge (Rives Road) this fish weir or fish dam has been dated to the 1300s and is still relatively intact. It's distinctive "V" shaped rock structure is best viewed at low water conditions. Native American structures of its type consist of stones piled in the bed of the river to form a low, V-shaped wall or dam usually extending from bank to bank with the apex of the V pointing downstream. The apex of the V was left open, and a basket was held there to trap fish as they swam with the current and were funneled into the basket, or driven downstream by a group of fishermen."

Beverly Yeager sent this to me after talking with Brian M. Williams, Education, Outreach, and Conservation Coordinator, Dan River Basin Association (www.danriver.org.) This site in 1974 joined the Virginia Register of Historic Places making it the oldest documented historical site in Henry County.

The first documented visit to the area that became Martinsville and Henry County was the surveyors from North Carolina and Virginia. Among them was William Byrd, who recorded his thoughts on the journey that ended along Peter's Creek in what is today neighboring Patrick County. Later, Peter Jefferson and Joshua Fry of Virginia along with other surveyors from North Carolina extended the line.

On October 12, 1728, Byrd wrote, "About four miles beyond the river Irvin, we forded Matrimony creek, called so by an unfortunate married man, because it was exceedingly noisy and impetuous. However, though the stream was clamorous, yet, like those women who make themselves plainest heard, it was likewise perfectly clear and unsullied. Still half a mile further we saw a small mountain, about five miles to the north-west of us, which we called the Wart, because it appeared no bigger than a wart, in comparison of the great mountains which hid their haughty heads in the clouds. We were not able to extend the line farther than five miles and one hundred and thirty five poles, not withstanding we began our march early in the morning, and did not encamp till it was almost dark..."

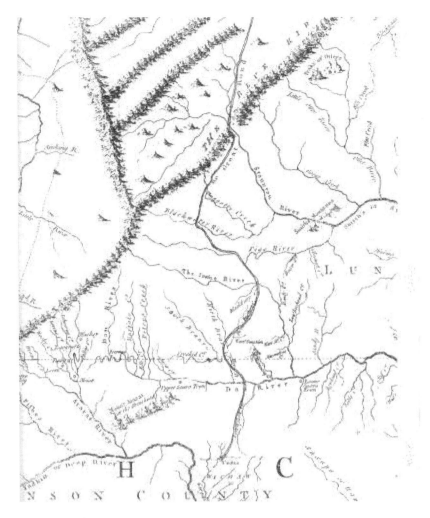

Getting to Martinsville before the days of the automobile was by horse or by foot across rivers without bridges, but by ford. In the Jefferson-Fry Map shown here drawn by Thomas Jefferson's father Peter and his fellow surveyor Joshua Fry shows the area now occupied by Martinsville. William Byrd's survey team named the Smith River, the Irvine or Irwin River. The dotted line shows the boundary between North Carolina and Virginia. Wart Mountain, Leatherwood, and Marrowbone Creeks are just some of the landmarks still in Henry County.

162

Driving into Martinsville on Business Route 220 from the south, you cannot miss the dam when crossing the bridge over the Smith River. "This landmark is a hydroelectric dam which provides energy needs for the City of Martinsville. The dam constructed in the 1920s and was in operation by 1924. Prior to this dam, the site was the location of a milldam. Very few communities built hydroelectric plants during this period - most were private. For industrial and technology buffs, the dam is stone gravity structure, 575 ft long, 32 ft high, and has a 32 ft head. A concrete cap and steel tainter gates control the flow and distribution of water flow. An adjoining concrete and brick powerhouse contains two vertical generating units with capacity of 1300 Kilowatts."

(Preceding photos courtesy of Elva Adams, Jerry Brock, Teddy Compton, and Doug Stegall.)

Chapter Eleven
Getting Around

Travel and tragic accidents still come together. Around 1890, a balloon came to Martinsville and set up in Oakwood Cemetery. Volunteers agreed to help, but when the signal to release the guide ropes came, one person, Archie Brown, did not let go either due to tangling or misunderstanding and floated up with the balloon several hundred feet until he fell to his death. The balloon traveled for nearly two hours before coming down east of town causing a mother and children to run to the woods.

Martinsville is the crossroads for many ways of travel. Highways 58 and 220 intersect the city. Coming from Virginia Beach to the Cumberland Gap, the east to west, Highway 58, variously known as the A. L. Philpott Highway or J. E. B. Stuart Highway brings four lanes of traffic through and around the "City Without Limits." Coming from Greensboro, North Carolina, going north to Roanoke, Virginia, 220 brings four lanes of traffic as well as the future path of Interstate 73 that many in Martinsville are working vigorously to bring to town.

Above, an Ox cart was a favored way of transportation along with horsepower. Below, Henry Stultz before 1920 delivered mail on Rural Free Delivery Number One with his horse and homemade wagon.

Watt H. Hairston driving his father, James T. W. "Watt" Hairston, in a 1908 Winston automobile along Main Street. Below, the same Winston Six was the first car in Martinsville and owned by Watt Hairston, who bought it in Roanoke, but went to Baltimore to pick it up. Left to right are Ben Townes, John Waynick, son of the Roanoke dealer, and Watt Hairston. A story about Hairston states that when pulled over for speeding, he paid double the fine because he would be speeding when he came back through. Another story states that Hairston was also the first automobile fatality in Henry County due to his driving.

Above, the first fire truck in Martinsville. Below, J. I. Shumate and Perry Saunders were involved in an accident not too far from the scene above on the Old River Hill Road, now Rt. 220, Memorial Boulevard. In the distance is a Hairston home, and is where DuPont Road turns right to the site of the nylon plant.

Above, driving in the courthouse square in 1912 are Dr.
George L. Houchins, Dr. Morton E. Hundley, Annie Minter,
Elizabeth Bondurant Hundley and John Armstrong Shackelford.
Below, the Stevens Family at the Watt Hairston Memorial Hospital.

In 1912, Dr. Morton E. Hundley and Dr. C. P. Kearfott driving the courthouse square in a Hudson.

Chapter Twelve
Hospitals

Above, Dr. James Moss Smith operated a hospital in his home, built in 1841, where the Martinsville Municipal Building sits today. He was the father of John Redd Smith, Sr. and grandfather of John Redd Smith, Jr. Union forces under William J. Palmer used the home during Stoneman's Raid in April 1865.

Dr. John P. Bing covered the history of these many hospitals in his book, *The Hands: A History of Hospitals in Martinsville and Henry County, Virginia.* Today, Memorial Hospital of Martinsville and Henry County, shown below, serves the region. Beginning in 1970 until sold in 2002, a local board operated the hospital. Funds from the sale went to form the Harvest Foundation, which funds many projects locally.

Above, Dr. Jesse M. Shackelford purchased the Shackelford Hospital, built by Dr. C. T. Womack in 1900, in 1921. Shackelford built a three-storey addition. Son, Dr. John Armstrong Shackelford operated the hospital until 1947. Below, the Watt Hairston Memorial Hospital located on the site of Liberty Fair Mall today, operated only a short time beginning in 1919 until it burned on March 7, 1920. Miss Anne Marshall Hairston lived in the home until her death in 1907 and then it was occupied by Watt H. Hairston until his death in 1916.

Operated as the Lucy Lester Hospital and the Broad Street Hotel, Dr. Morton Eldridge Hundley began practicing here in 1919. Chartered on January 13, 1920, this structure had ten rooms, three private rooms, and two wards with five to six patients each. One was for "Negroes" and became the dining room when the structure became a hotel.

It was not a racetrack, but the Henry County Memorial Hospital located today near the Dutch Inn in Collinsville. It operated from 1941 until 1948 when it became the Hughes Apartment Building. Below, Martinsville General Hospital operated from 1946 until 1970. Located at 15 Starling Avenue, it is now the site of the Virginia Museum of Natural History and the First Baptist Church in downtown Martinsville. It operated as the Kennedy House Apartments after being a hospital.

Chapter Thirteen
Those Who Fought Fire

     Jerry Brock, Chief of the Martinsville Fire Department from 1997 until 2006, in February 1980 leaving the Pannill Knitting Company fire. Chief Brock, one of thirteen men to hold the position of Fire Chief, shared many of the photos included in this chapter. Relatives of J. E. B. Stuart started Pannill Knitting, one of the many textile firms that once dominated the area. (All the photos in this chapter are courtesy of Jerry Brock.)

This image of Martinsville Fire Chief Clay E. Easterly (1956-1968) with Educator Reverend R. T. Anderson shows a group of African-American students before desegregation of the Virginia Public Schools. The volunteer fire department first organized in 1891 with two 500 feet hoses made a serious effort to educate children about fire safety and prevention.

This image shows Fire Marshall Frank L. Draper, Jr. in November 1980 as he enters the Specialty Packing Company fire. Beginning in 1949, the Fire Marshall position trained the volunteer firefighters and educated the public with fire prevention programs. The volunteers received the same training as the paid firefighters.

This image is of J. Lloyd Gregory, Martinsville Fire Chief from 1968 until 1988, as the water from a firefight falls down on him in downtown Martinsville. Presently, the fire department operates two stations with thirty full-time personnel, thirteen part-time, twenty-seven volunteer fire fighters, and an eighteen-member honor guard.

This haunting image comes from the L. and F. Repair fire on Chestnut Street. From Samuel Morgan in 1891 to Kenneth Draper beginning in 2007, thirteen men have served as Chief of the Martinsville Fire Department including J. D. Aaron, P. S. Ford, J. H. Pharis, J. R. Henley, James E. Minter, Clay E. Easterly, J. Lloyd Gregory, W. Lewis Reeves, Jerry Brock, and Clarence Monday.

Sparky, the firedog, is still the mascot of the Martinsville Fire Department. He was a fixture in parades and events in the area spreading the word about fire safety and prevention started by the Fire Marshall. Jerry Brock says that social activity was always a big part of the Martinsville Volunteer Fire Company. In this photo from the 1950s among others are Mable and John Ingram, Avis and Ed David, C. K. Sparrow, Sam Ingram, John Redd Penn, Juanita Warren, Leslie Nance, Ben Ramsey, and Dutch Shilbe with child.

182

Above and on the preceding page, each summer the
Martinsville Volunteer Fire Company held a fund raiser known as the
Fireman's Bazaar at the Brown Street Field near the present location
of Ellsworth and Market Streets in the 1960s. Below are the
"Milkmen" of the Martinsville Volunteer Fire Company in the mid
1960s. Front row are Carl Cooper, B. D. Norman, Leonard Hurrell,
Bill Kochersperger, Jack Bouldin, and Jim Slice. Second row are C.
K. Sparrow, Ira Asbury, O. K. Chapple, Page Brockenbrough, Boyd
Grey, Richard Prillaman, Bruce Gilbert, J. D. Spencer, Frank Warren,
Garland Lovell, and Jim Spencer. The back row includes two
unknowns with Jim Staton, Arnold Prillaman, William Lovell, Ernest
Lassiter, Ray Haley, and Buck Wells.

Above is Gladys Brown Wyatt, the secretary to the Martinsville City Manager and the Volunteer Fire Company. Below are the ladies of the Auxiliary of the Martinsville Fire Department.

In the early 1950s, civil defense was part of the preparation for the Cold War. The Martinsville Fire Department was the lead agency in the event of a "catastrophic event." The motorcyclists above took part in a planning exercise. Below, Chief J. Lloyd Gregory in the late 1970s was shown previously in this chapter. Chief Gregory passed away during the preparation of this book. The Martinsville Fire Department Headquarters now bears his name. He like the men and women who work every day to protect the citizens of Martinsville should never be taken for granted.

Chapter Fourteen
A Drive Down Church Street

 Two-way traffic traverses Church Street in this 1951 image with the U. S. Post Office on the right with flags at half-mast and Eagles's Coffee Shop on the left. Looking east towards the Thomas Jefferson Hotel beside a Pure filling station, the old Henry County Courthouse is one block to the left.

Church Street Looking North, Martinsville, Va.

Two postcards show many landmarks along Church Street from nearly one hundred years ago in downtown Martinsville.

Above, Church Street in the 1940s. Below, a view of Church Street from 1953 Martinsville looking west shows one-way traffic as people make their way around. Before the days of strip malls, all in one stores, megaplex theaters, and fast food, people specialized in stores and lunch at the local café, catching a movie while shopping downtown and knowing the lost art of parallel parking. (Courtesy of Jerry Brock.)

Often the past is not as clear as one hopes. Even photos like our memories are grainy as these two images from Church Street taken fifty years apart and fifty and one hundreds years ago.

Looking west on Church Street above include the H. B. Hundley residence on the right followed by the office of Dr. R. R. Lee, then the ice cream parlor of Morris Praeger. On the left is the home of T. C. Matthews, then the home of H. S. Teague, which became the Shackelford Hospital and then the home of Dr. J. A. Shackelford, next his office and then the Post Office.

Looking east on Church Street at the left is the home of Dr. J. W. Simmons with his office on the left facing his home, then the home of R. E. Tuggle and his sisters, then R. F. McMillion's home, which the Lee Telephone Company building replaced. Next was the First Methodist Church. The home of Henry Clay Lester is to the left in the background of this image, which later was the home of Rives S. Brown, Sr. The houses on the left at the end of the street belonged to H. C. Gravely and Pannill Rucker, which became the home of Rives Brown, Sr. and William Letcher Pannill, now belonging to Christ Episcopal Church.

Spectators at the corner of Church and Walnut streets looked east in downtown Martinsville as a parade including Esso gas trucks heads east. Martinsville named for General Joseph Martin, a hero of the American Revolution, is unusual because it is an independent city declared in 1928 and remained the county seat of Henry County until 1996. (Courtesy of Jerry Brock.)

A view of Church Street in Martinsville after a snow taken in 1966. This area known as "Camera Corner" had camera, bookstores along with Wards, Faggs, and Leggett's. (Courtesy of Elva Adams, www.myhenrycounty.com)

A trip down memory lane in downtown Martinsville might include a show at the Roxy Theater or shopping for hardware at the Advance Store. While below, the corner drugstore, J. C. Penny, and the Thomas Jefferson Hotel offer services to residents and visitors.

Above is the corner of Bridge and Church Streets and below is the corner of Broad and Church Street.

Chapter Fifteen
Reason To Believe

In tough economic times such as Martinsville experienced with the loss of textile, furniture, and the closure of the DuPont plant, it speaks to the character of the people of the "City Without Limits" that taking care of those in need is still strong. A recent article in the New Yorker magazine portrayed Martinsville as a "Ghost Town," but this chapter contains images of recent efforts that show this positive side of Martinsville and those who believe there is a strong reason to believe that prosperous times are again in the future.

There is the Grace Network, a non-profit organization that assists clients in crisis with essential life needs. They help with finances, food, and other programs. Each year they turn the empty lot at First Baptist Church into a pumpkin patch. The proceeds from the pumpkin sale go to feed people in the community and help prevent them from being without power or heat. The image is eighty volunteers from all over the community that came out to help unload the truck and set up with patch. Volunteers range from age of one to the oldest about 80. You can see their website www.gracenetworkmhc.org.

New College Institute conducts higher education classes in the wonderful old buildings around the old Henry County Courthouse Square in downtown Martinsville making a striking contrast between a rich history and the modernity and forward momentum of the city. The first classroom building, the former Shumate-Jesse Furniture showroom, is located adjacent to the historic Henry County Courthouse.

NCI held a graduate recognition ceremony in 2009 for the 86 graduates who received degrees in the first three years. Here are some of them including Ashley Smith, Emily Clark, Emily Harrell, Heather Hoffman, Michelle Barker, then Virginia Governor Timothy M. Kaine, Lance Janney, Roxanne Collins, and Dr. Gary Nelson faculty-in-residence and program coordinator for Longwood University's program for elementary school teachers.

Encouraging future generations is the mission of the Boys and Girls Clubs of the Blue Ridge. Here are the Youth of the Year finalists Tyler Allen, Kenya Moore, and Devante Martin holding the envelope. Devante, a fifteen-year-old freshman at Martinsville High School, received a $500 scholarship from Carter Bank and Trust for being Youth of the Year for 2010 and represented the local club at the state level. Kenya is also a freshman at MHS has a black belt in karate and is in the marching band. Tyler is an eighth grader at Martinsville Middle School, where he plays baseball and is in the Junior Beta Club. All three gave speeches. Below from left to right are, Robert McClure, Xavier Savannah, Helen Nguyen, Lois Christensen, Isaac Cavero, and Jasmyn Carter involved in a community service project. Learn more about the Boys and Girls Clubs of the Blue Ridge at www.bgcmhc.org. (Courtesy of Anne Frazier.)

Above, a grant from the Save American Treasurers includes the Martinsville Henry County Courthouse, shown here on April 16, 2010, as part of the "This Treasure Matters" campaign. Below, the Harvest Foundation breaks ground at the Bassett Historical Center after giving a matching grant of $200,000. The foundation distributes money in Martinsville and Henry County from proceeds from the sale of the hospital.

"The Martinsville Historic District encompasses a 45-acre district encompassing 96 historically contributing buildings with architecture reflective of a number of architectural styles: Federal, Romanesque, Colonial Revival, and Classic Revival dating to between 1791 and 1948 and include Commercial Style, International Style, Art Decco, and Others. The district joined both the Virginia Landmarks Register and National Register of Historic Places in 1998. Nomination for the district highlighted three distinct significant dates for meeting the criteria for listing: 1791, 1824, and 1873. The Martinsville Uptown Revitalization Association (MURA) a Main Street Community Revitalization Program - offers a Walking Tour Guide of the area." www.martinsvilleuptown.com

The "Chair" came to Martinsville in 2010, donated by Bassett Furniture, who built it eight years earlier. Placed in the parking lot along Church Street, the chair is "an icon in the local Deep Roots campaign, which will use the area's furniture, textile, and motorsports legacies as a springboard for tourism and revitalization efforts."

As mentioned earlier, you can tell a lot about a community by the way it treats the least among its population including its animal population. The Martinsville-Henry County SPCA recently opened the Shelley Frith Drane Adoption Center south of town off Business 220 that includes a dog park and walking trail. www.spcamhc.org.

The Last Chapter
Full Circle
A Personal Journey Through Martinsville's History

    For this author, Henry County history began with a visit to
Beaver Creek, the stately home of the Hairstons, with educator,
genealogist, and historian Ophus Eugene Pilson in the 1980s. Like
many people who encountered O. E. Pilson, you remember how he
shared his knowledge of local history. Carrying this author around in
his blue Chevrolet led to many sites and stories about the history of
Martinsville and Henry County.

    Today, Worth Harris Carter, Jr.'s Carter Bank and Trust owns
Beaver Creek. Before that Plastic Surgeon Dr. J. Michael Bestler
owned the home purchasing it from the Covington Family.

    It was at Beaver Creek that West Point Cadet James Ewell
Brown "Jeb" Stuart courted young Elizabeth Perkins "Bettie"
Hairston in the 1850s. His letters to the young lady survive in the
Southern Historical Collection at UNC-Chapel Hill.

    Ophus Eugene Pilson, an educator from Patrick County, came
to live in Ridgeway amassing a huge collection of historical and
genealogical information before his death in 1999. Mr. Pilson's
collection was so large that he purchased the house next door to keep
it. Today, the Bassett Historical Center contains his collection in an
entire room dedicated to it.

O. E. Pilson

Elizabeth "Bettie" Perkins Hairston, the daughter of Marshall Hairston grew up at Beaver Creek Plantation north of Martinsville. Her family dominated Henry County agriculture and politics in the nineteenth century. Her grandfather, George, gave fifty acres of land for the second Henry County Courthouse located uptown in Martinsville. George was one of the largest land and slaveholders in Virginia. The original Beaver Creek was the second Hairston home in Henry County (Marrowbone was first). Built in 1776 by George Hairston on a "Kings Grant" of 30,000 acres, the family rebuilt the house in 1837 after a fire. Later in the 1800s, they added two wings to the home. Other owners added a third wing with a sun porch. Dr. J. Michael Bestler operated a plastic surgery practice in this home in the twentieth century. Today Carter Bank and Trust owns the building and grounds. Patriot Centre Industrial Park and Patrick Henry Community College now occupy part of the huge land holdings that once saw labor of the slaves owned by the Hairstons.

Bettie and Watt Hairston

James Ewell Brown "Jeb" Stuart left in 1854 and right in 1862.

One of those who walked among the thirty-foot high boxwoods of Beaver Creek Plantation was James Ewell Brown "Jeb" Stuart shown in this 1850 photo on the left, as his cousin Elizabeth Perkins "Bettie" Hairston knew him. Stuart graduated from the United States Military Academy at West Point and went on to a career in the U. S. Army and then in the Civil War as cavalry commander under Robert E. Lee, in the 1862 photo on the right.

Bettie and J. E. B. shared the same ancestor. Elizabeth Perkins Letcher Hairston of Pittsylvania County married William Letcher in 1778 and moved to the Ararat River in present day Patrick County, but was then Henry County. When Tories killed Letcher in 1780, Elizabeth returned home with George Hairston, who married her and had a dozen children. Among these children was Marshall Hairston, the father of Bettie.

J. E. B. Stuart descends from the only child of William Letcher and Elizabeth Perkins Letcher Hairston, Bethenia, who married David Pannill. Their two children were Elizabeth Letcher Pannill and William Letcher Pannill. The latter is the progenitor of the family that started Pannill Knitting Company and the former is the mother of the famous Civil War General, who came to court his cousin Bettie at Beaver Creek.

Remembering the legacy of history passed to me through Mr. Pilson and bringing my journey through Martinsville's history full circle, I end with a personal story. On May 3, 2006, I took a young lady named Ashley to Beaver Creek, twenty-one years after I should have met her. Not everything in life works out the way you want it or should, but I remember something I started my last book with. A quote from a good friend, Beverly Millner, who wrote, "Many of the children born today really have no reference point. You really don't know yourself until you know something of your history. For the most part, we are concerned about our future generations. If a child knows about where she came from and how important she is, that is going to do a lot for her values, her destiny in life. It will give her the vision she needs to make it through all the various obstacles in life today."

I told Ashley about Bettie Hairston and the young West Point Lieutenant, who courted his distant cousin at this house. I told her about Elizabeth Perkins Letcher Hairston, who saw her first husband gunned down at Stuart's Birthplace in my hometown, Ararat, Virginia, because he was a Patriot in the American Revolution. I told her about George Hairston, who came and brought Elizabeth back home and married her.

We spent the afternoon together. I took her to the Bassett Historical Center and showed her my collection of material there along with her new family genealogy book on my family. Kenney Kirkman took some photos of us together that day. One of our first first photos together near the Civil War books at the Bassett Historical Center will be one of the last images of Martinsville and Henry County. I hope you enjoyed this book and if you have images of Martinsville or Henry County to share, please contact this author or the Bassett Historical Center.

"...Two drifters off to see the world. There's such a lot of world to see. We're after the same rainbow's end-- waiting 'round the bend, my huckleberry friend, Moon River and me." –Johnny Mercer

Websites

Martinsville Tourism www.visitmartinsville.com

MURA www.martinsvilleuptown.com

SVAC www.southernvirginiaartisancenter.org

Martinsville Speedway www.martinsvillespeedway.com

Bassett Historical Center www.bassetthistoricalcenter.com

Fayette Street Historical Area Initiative
www.aaheritageva.org/special%20projects/martinsville.php

Piedmont Arts Association www.piedmontarts.org

Virginia Museum of Natural History www.vmnh.net

Martinsville-Henry County Economic Development
www.yesmartinsville.com

My Martinsville/Henry County www.myhenrycounty.com

City of Martinsville www.ci.martinsville.va.us

Henry County Virginia www.henrycountyva.gov

Dan River Basin Organization www.danriver.org

Boys and Girls Club www.bgcmhc.org

Grace Network www.gracenetworkmhc.org

Martinsville Henry County SPCA www.spcamhc.org

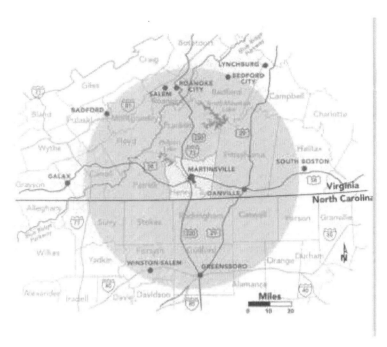

Acknowledgements

Thanks to retired Martinsville Fire Chief Jerry Brock, who shared his incredible collection of photos about the town he served protecting the lives of the people from fire. Meeting him and learning of his love of history made this book more than worth the many hours scanning and working on the enclosed images.

Thanks to Elva Adkins Adams, who shared her images from her website www.myhenrycounty.com and her love of history and the area she lives. Her support over the years has been instrumental in my work on Martinsville and Henry County history.

Thanks to the following for sharing their images for this book: Teddy Compton, Anne Copeland, Anne Frazier, Virgil Goode, Deborah Hodges, Kenney Kirkman, David Minter, Bill Moore, Harold Smith, Douglas Stegall, the Asheville Postcard Company, and the Martinsville Bulletin.

Patricia Ross and Debbie Hall read the manuscript of this book and gave many useful critiques and information that made it better. As always, all mistakes are this author's.

The Bassett Historical Center of the Blue Ridge Regional Library most of the images and assistance beyond the call of duty in the making of this work. The library, my research "Home" receives a portion of the royalty from this book. So by purchasing this book you not only enjoy the history of Martinsville, but you assist in the preservation of that history at the "Best Little Library in Virginia."

This image shows Martinsville once had "The South's Largest Mirror Plant." This 1939 token is from the Virginia Mirror Company. Founded in 1913, the company operates today a 176,000-foot plant in Martinsville and 110,000-foot facility in Ridgeway in southern Henry County. While textiles and chemicals have left, the glass and mirror business remains. (Courtesy of Douglas Stegall.)

The home of George Tilden "Cap'n Til" Lester and his second wife, Lottie, who along with the children of his first marriage lived at this house on Starling Avenue.

Index

C

Cahill, 29
Caldwell, 90
Campbell, 29, 90
Carper, 30
Carter, 29, 38, 65, 67, 93, 95,
    127, 130, 195, 199, 200
Casey, 92
Cassady, 95
Cavero, 195
Chambliss, 28
Chatmoss, 19, 88
Chewning, 39
Chief Tassel Building, 53, 70
Childress, 29, 38
Childs, 8
Chittum, 118
Christ Episcopal, 76, 77, 124,
    138, 189
Christensen, 195
Church Street, 5, 22, 33, 35,
    47, 52, 60, 81, 87, 97, 122,
    124, 156, 185, 186, 187,
    188, 189, 190, 192, 197
Civil War, 4, 6, 8, 10, 15, 41,
    77, 123, 201, 202
Clark, 29, 142, 194
Claudville, 66
Clay, 19, 119, 127, 142, 149,
    178, 179, 189
Claybon, 138
Clingenpeel, 127
Cole, 121
Coleman, 41
Collins, 194
Collinsville, 13, 18, 127, 176
Compton, 90, 166, 205
Concannon, 92
Cooper, 131, 182
Copeland, 89, 205
courthouse, 13, 46, 47, 48, 59,
    63, 66, 74, 97, 99, 100, 101,
    102, 105, 106, 107, 108,
    111, 112, 114, 171, 172
Craigshead, 95
Cubine, 39
Curlee, 91

D

Dan River, 7, 24, 160, 203
Danville, 28, 83, 94, 142, 143,
    146, 147
Davis, 23, 30, 35, 38, 42, 43,
    86
Descales, 138
DeShazo, 29
Dick and Willie, 28, 143, 146,
    147
Dillard, 29, 31, 34, 57, 59, 64,
    127, 133
Doss, 24, 32
Doyle, 90
Draper, 22, 91, 118, 178, 179
Drewry, 66, 93, 125, 127, 138
Dudley, 69, 79
Duncan, 32
DuPont, 25, 54, 71, 90, 91,
    119, 126, 170, 193
Dutch Inn, 176
Dyer, 23, 130

E

Eanes, 30, 32
Earles, 149, 158
Easterly, 178, 179
Edison, 129
Eggleston, 21, 53
Ehly, 90
English, 75, 88, 92, 93, 127,
    141
Epperson, 154

F

Faggs, 89, 190

Sons of Confederate Veterans,
112
Soyars, 41
Sparrow, 93, 180, 182
SPCA, 198, 203
Spencer, 26, 29, 59, 91, 182
Stanford, 99
Stanley, 11, 125
Starling Avenue, 22, 36, 37,
69, 77, 176, 196, 206
Stegall, 111, 166, 205, 206
Stevens, 171
Stevenson, 118
Stiles, 106
Stone, 30, 127, 128
Stoneman, 123, 173
Strickland, 91
Stringfellow, 124
Stuart, 4, 6, 15, 28, 77, 112,
124, 132, 146, 167, 177,
199, 201, 202
Stuart, James Ewell Brown
"Jeb", 4, 6
Stultz, 32, 75, 127, 168
Summers, 29
Swanson, 34, 66, 95, 108
Sweatshirt Capital of the
World, 54, 78

T

Taylor, 29, 34, 42, 91, 138
Teague, 22, 29, 31, 189
Terry, 128, 154
Thomas, 1, 2, 4, 6, 8, 9, 21,
75, 80, 84, 123, 125, 128,
129, 130, 131, 135, 161,
185, 191
Thompson, 32, 41
Thorton, 60
Tilley, 90
Townes, 85, 102, 169
Truman, 21, 120

Tuggle, 29, 38, 43, 189
Tultex, 11, 79, 80, 82, 111
Tunstall, 41
Turner, 32, 39, 93

U

United Daughters of the
Confederacy, 99
University of Virginia, 94
Urezetti, 92

V

Vickers, 80
Vipperman, 128
Virginia Landmarks Register,
60, 197
Virginia Museum of Natural
History, 49, 50, 176, 203
Virginia Tech, 6, 94, 96
Vogler, 29

W

Wade, 90
Walker, 9, 29, 78, 82
Wampler, 30
Wards, 190
Warner, 130
Warren, 31, 34, 180, 182
Webb, 43
Webster, 28
Wells, 29, 99, 182
Whitaker, 95
White, 35, 90, 118, 122
Whitener, 45
Whittle, 87, 137, 138
Williams, 67, 80, 133, 160
Willis, 25
Wilson, 38, 39, 140
Wingfield, 91
Witten, 79, 80
WMVA, 40
Womack, 67, 174

It is not Gene Simmons of the rock band KISS, but Henry County Administrative Assistant Jennifer Gregory, a member of the KISS Army. Afterall, Martinsville is a city without limits.